The 100 Best Bulbs

A PRACTICAL ENCYCLOPEDIA

The 100 Best Bulbs

A PRACTICAL ENCYCLOPEDIA

PREVIOUSLY PUBLISHED AS PART OF *THE 400 BEST GARDEN PLANTS*

ELVIN McDONALD

RANDOM HOUSE   NEW YORK

A Packaged Goods Incorporated Book

Published in the United States by
Random House, Inc.
201 E. 50th Street
New York, NY 10022

Conceived and produced by
Packaged Goods Incorporated
276 Fifth Avenue, New York, NY 10001
A Quarto Company

Text and photography by Elvin McDonald
Designed by Yasuo Kubota, Kubota & Bender

Library of Congress Cataloging-in-Publication Data
The 100 best bulbs: a practical encyclopedia
Elvin McDonald.

p. cm.

Includes index.
ISBN 0-679-76029-6
1. Plants, Ornamental—Encyclopedias. 2. Plants,
Ornamental—Pictorial works. 3. Gardening—
Encyclopedias. 4. Gardening—Pictorial works.
I. Title. II. Title: The one hundred best bulbs.
III. Title: A practical encyclopedia.

SB407.M26 1995
35.9—dc20 94-35385

Random House website address: http://www.randomhouse.com/
Color separations by Hong Kong Scanner Arts Int'l Ltd.
Printed and bound in Singapore by Khai Wah-Ferco Pte. Ltd.
98765432
First Edition

Acknowledgments

Dedicated to Marta Hallett

Thanks to the home team, pals, and friends, particularly:

Kristen Schilo, editor; Mary Forsell, copyeditor;
Sarah Krall, assistant editor; Yasuo Kubota, designer;
Tatiana Ginsberg, production manager; Amy Detjen,
assistant production editor; Catherine San Filippo,
proofreader; Lillien Waller, helping hand; Carla Glasser, agent;
Douglas Askew, research; Tom Osborn, driver/gardener;
Rosalind Creasy, focalizer; James R. Bailey, neighbor;
Janis Blackschleger, telekineticist; Diane Ofner,
gardening student; JoAnn Trial, scientist, and Don Trial,
teacher; R. Michael Lee, architect; Charles Gulick,
gardener; Michael Berryhill, poet; Linda Starr, head
coach; Hila Paldi, body coach; Mark Inabnit, Publisher
and Editor-in-Chief, *Houston Life*; David Walker,
Editorial Director, *Houston Life*; Catherine Beason, angel
unaware; Maria Moss, Executive Editor, *Houston Life*;
David Warren, artist/gardenmaker; Audrey Scachnow,
tweak expressionist; Christy Barthelme, envisionary; Tino
and Richard, Stark Cleaning Services; Tony Williams, yard
man; Dan Twyman, pruner; and Leslie Williams, cheering.

Elvin McDonald
Houston, Texas
January 1, 1997

Contents

The one hundred plants that appear in these colorful pages represent my pick of the crop as a lifelong gardener and horticultural journalist. They are far from being the only "best" plants. Some vast families and categories certainly deserve more attention. Most assuredly, I am already growing the plants and assembling the photography for a sequel. One of the most wonderful aspects of gardening is that we can never know all of the plants. For this reason, dedicated gardeners will always experience the thrill of the hunt, the excitement upon discovering a flower or plant more beguiling than could have been imagined.

How to Read an Entry

Within this book, plants appear in alphabetical order by botanical genus name. If you know only the plant's common name, look for it in the Index. The botanical name and its suggested pronunciation are followed by the common name or names, many of which are interchangeable, and then by the plant's family name, appearing first in botanical Latin and finally in English. For example, plants of the genus *Dietes* (botanical name) are commonly referred to as African iris (common name). They are members of the Iridaceae (botanical family name), or iris family (common family name).

Within the entries, species names sometimes appear, where applicable. For instance, in the *Leucojum*, or snowflake, entry, the species names *L. vernalis, L. aestivum,* and *L. autumnale* appear. All are broadly referred to as snowflake. Oftentimes, species do not have common names and, as a result, are known in the plant trade only by their botanical names.

In all, one hundred different plants are pictured in this volume, yet many more are actually named, a resource unto itself for tracking down worthwhile species and cultivars.

Within each entry, there is also a guide for cultivation:

Height/habit: Despite the inexactness of horticulture and botanical differences, I sum up here as much as can be said about a genus in as few words as possible.

Leaves: Many plants are appreciated for their foliage as much as—or even more so—than their flowers. Here I provide a succinct description of leaf shapes and characteristics.

Flowers: Dimensions, arrangement, and color and fragrance characteristics are noted.

Season: The plant's high season appears here.

When to plant: I have used the phrase "Set out transplants when available" for nearly all plants in the book. In other words, if a gardener shops regularly for plants, both through mail order and locally (at nurseries, garden centers, and plant auctions held by public gardens), they will be delivered or sold at approximately the correct planting time for that person's hardiness zone. Containerization, lightweight growing mediums, remarkably efficient distribution, and computerization have revolutionized the plant business. Yes, there are still plants shipped at the wrong time and local retailers who sell inappropriate choices, but on the whole, the system works.

I have also provided each plant's tolerance for cold and heat according to zone, as it appears on the United States Department of Agriculture's Plant Hardiness Zone Map (see page 112). (This information can also appear under "Season," if applicable.) However, please note that the U.S.D.A. map has traditionally been based on cold tolerance, not heat. Now the billion-dollar gardening industry is working to generate maps and zone awareness for heat as well as cold, also taking into account the relative dryness or wetness of a particular climate. To establish heat tolerance zones for this book, I have used a variety of references, including the catalogs of Louisiana Nursery, Wayside Gardens, and Yucca Do Nursery (see Resources). I have also consulted the books listed in the Bibliography, especially *A Garden Book for Houston* and *Hortica.* When in doubt, ask a neighbor who gardens for details about your hardiness zone. There are lots of variables and a host of gardeners who like nothing better than trying to succeed with a plant that is not rated for their zone.

Light: To prosper, most plants need strong light or some sun, in a site that affords air movement. Here, I provide specific light or shade requirements.

Soil: Most plants need well-drained soil that is kept evenly moist to on the dry side. There are rainy seasons when gardens are wet for long periods of time. If water stands for more than a few hours in your yard, this does not bode well for gardening—unless you are undertaking a water or bog garden. There are also dry seasons, and gardeners today generally subscribe to the concept of Xeriscaping: not to set in motion any garden that will require undue irrigation during normal times of drought.

Fertilizer: Generally speaking, 5-10-5 and 15-30-15 are good for flowering-fruiting plants. Timed-release 14-14-14 is an all-purpose, long-serving (up to a whole season from one application) fertilizer for a wide variety of plants. For acid-loving plants, choose 30-10-10 or chelated iron. Careful, consistent application of these or entirely organic fertilizers will result in vigorous growth.

Propagation: Lots of gardeners favor propagation over just about everything else done in the course of a gardening season. It is fun to see little seeds sprout and roots take hold from brown-looking cuttings.

Uses: Under this heading, each plant's strong points are discussed, though you the gardener may find your own unique usages.

As much as I can provide detailed information about the art of gardening, you will be your own best teacher, a philosophy stated most eloquently in this old garden verse:

> *If you seek answers,*
> *leave your questions*
> *outside the garden gate.*

Elvin McDonald
Houston, Texas   January 1, 1997

Chapter One
The Bulb Garden

Flowers that grow from corms, tubers, rhizomes, thickened roots, and true bulbs all fall under the umbrella heading of bulbs. Most gardeners consider bulbs to be the most supreme among all flowering plants. So varied are they in size, color, and blooming periods, bulbs alone can easily comprise an elaborate, multiseason garden. At the same time, bulbs fit in nicely with the overall gardening scheme.

Bulbs grow equally well in the ground and in containers, and gardeners will find types for all kinds of climates. Some are evergreen, but it is the general habit of bulbs to return to the ground for one season yearly, either in winter or summer, depending on each plant's built-in timetable.

Planning and Designing the Bulb Garden

Bulbs growing on their own in the wild form irregularly shaped colonies. Mimicking nature and planting in informal drifts, the gardener can create such a charming scene in his or her own garden, perhaps on a grassy bank. Another possibility is to design formal beds, perhaps edged with dwarf boxwood or dwarf yaupon holly, and to fill them with different bulbs in season. Such a scheme entails discarding each successive round of bulbs when its season has finished.

Of course, many gardeners also choose to fill their beds with bulbs in spring and annuals in summer. By the time the annuals finish in early fall, it is time to plant another round of bulbs. Bulbs also look quite lovely when planted among ground cover plants so that when they're done blooming, the area will not look bare. Remember to plant low-growing bulbs in places where they'll be clearly visible, reserving the taller types for the back of the garden.

Another aesthetic—and practical—design tip to keep in mind is that spring bulbs are uniquely suited to growing in the company of deciduous trees; the bulbs usually bloom and grow leaves before the trees leaf out. The trees have a way of sucking up any extra moisture in summer, which is a boon to resting bulbs. Whether you live in a wet or dry climate, also consider using raised planting beds for bulbs. This makes gardening a lot easier in the long run and gives better results with most kinds of plants.

Soil Preparation

Bulbs adapt to various soil conditions, from soggy or boglike to quite dry. Study the description for each bulb you wish to grow (see Chapter Two). Cannas and crinums are examples of bulbous plants that grow and bloom in boggy conditions, even standing in water. Tulips, hyacinths, and daffodils and other narcissi are examples of bulbs that need a good supply of moisture from the time roots start expanding in fall until the leaves start yellowing naturally after bloom the following spring or early summer. Thereafter, it is beneficial to keep them quite dry, perhaps even stored out of the ground, for three or four months.

Before you plant bulbs, you need to dig and turn over the soil—at least to the depth of a spade—and clear away any weeds or other debris. Add a top-dressing of organic fertilizer and up to 6 inches (15 centimeters) of well-rotted compost. After you've tilled all of this together, the bed is ready for planting.

Buying and Planting Bulbs

Bulbs are sold in all seasons, both locally and through catalogs. When purchasing them, remember that, generally speaking, the larger the bulb, the bigger the blossoms. Just as with buying fruit, steer clear of bulbs that are too soft and mushy or seem to have moldy or bruised areas. On the other hand, if a bulb's outer skin is loose or torn, it is not necessarily damaged—this could even be a sign that root growth will be accelerated.

With all this in mind, it's time to plant the garden. The so-called Dutch, or spring, bulbs are planted in the fall, before the ground freezes in colder regions, up to around the first of the year in the South, in zone 9 and warmer. Narcissi, crocuses, hyacinths, tulips, Dutch irises, and scillas all belong to this category. One loose rule of thumb with spring bulbs is that they should be planted twice as deep as they are long, but check the descriptions in Chapter Two for precise measurements before planting.

Then there are the tender, or summer, bulbs, such as gladioli, dahlias, tuberoses, and tigridias. Northern gardeners traditionally plant them in the spring for summer blooms. Before the ground seriously begins to freeze in the fall, they dig them up and store them indoors. Plant summer bulbs at specific depths according to their needs, not based on the size of the bulb. Consult Chapter Two for specifics.

To plant bulbs, dig a hole to the specified depth, and be sure to loosen the soil under the bulbs as well. Cover with soil and water well.

Caring for Bulbs Throughout the Seasons

Despite the way they look, always bear in mind that bulbs are living things. Protect them from temperature extremes and be especially careful of their well-being at any time they are out of the ground. Spring-flowering bulbs, in particular, are quite vulnerable to high temperatures and direct sunshine, especially in a poorly ventilated room. Keep them well protected before planting, stored at a temperature below 60°F (15°C), perhaps in a well-ventilated closet in an open cardboard box. Keep all bulbs away from fruit before planting or during storing periods, as they are damaged by ethylene, released by the ripening fruit.

If the bulb is frost-sensitive, growing it in a pot is often the solution. Also, if the bulb needs a season of cold in order to bloom, chilling in the refrigerator is an option—provided it is kept away from fruit, as mentioned above.

At the other end of the bulb season, after flowering finishes, it is an absolute necessity to allow the foliage to grow out and complete its natural season. In many bulbous plants the leaves eventually turn yellow and die to the ground. It is at this point that the plants can be removed without harming their ability to bloom for the coming season. In general, spring-flowering bulbs can stay in the ground year-round (which encourages them to naturalize, especially crocuses, low-growing daffodils, snowdrops, and scillas), while summer-flowering bulbs should be dug up and stored in any climate where there is frost.

When any kind of bulb is resting, think of it not so much as being dormant but semidormant. Adequate fresh air circulation is important to prevent disease problems with such bulbs, and so is maintaining a state of dampness sufficient to prevent harmful drying-out, but not to the point of encouraging rot. With the exception of spring-flowering bulbs, which like a cooler temperature, most bulbs can be stored in a well-ventilated closet at temperatures of around 65–70°F (18–21°C).

A word about propagation: bulbs that bloom in spring are usually divided in summer or fall; bulbs that bloom in summer can be divided in the spring. Many bulbs never need to be divided, except for the purpose of propagation. Others start to die out in the center of the clump and stop blooming. This is a sign that digging and dividing are in order during or immediately following the next resting period.

To propagate bulbs by division, dig them up with a sharpshooter, garden spade, or trowel. Bulblets approximately the size of the bulbs originally planted can be removed and planted separately. Smaller ones may be set in groups of at least three or rowed out in a nursery bed for growing a year or two before being planted in a garden spot.

Bulbs that are content in a location will often colonize, spreading by offsets and sometimes by self-sown seedlings. Seeds of bulb flowers—especially not of the highly hybridized Dutch tulips, daffodils, and hyacinths—don't always come true, but the progeny is certainly fun to watch. Such kinds as the rain lilies—zephyranthes and habranthus, for example—seed profusely. They will take root quite nicely in well-prepared garden beds, either permitted to dry and drop seed where they will or harvested just before the capsule dries and breaks open, then planted within a month in shallow drills of moist soil. Friends will appreciate any extras.

The seeds of some bulbs planted one year may not germinate until the following spring or early summer. This is particularly true of the hardy types that need cold temperatures in winter, such as tulips, narcissi, and many of the true lilies (*Lilium*) and daylilies (*Hemerocallis*).

Essential Tools

Bulbs can be planted with a trowel or garden spade. There are hand-held bulb planters on the market but they do not work as handily as one might hope. A variation with a longer handle designed to be used with the feet works much better. When naturalizing fall-planted spring bulbs, such as crocus and winter aconite, you can use a dibble or crowbar to open up holes efficiently.

Year-round Gardening Calendar

Make note of the bulbs you like, then organize them according to recommended planting times. Write these various dates in your regular datebook/organizer or on a wall calendar. That way they serve as constant reminders of upcoming planting dates and also of bulbs that you'll need to obtain from a specialist or pick up at a local garden center. Here is a calendar of seasonal reminders:

SPRING:

Till and prepare soil in garden beds.

Replant summer bulbs stored over the winter after danger of frost has passed.

Divide bulbs in early spring, before blooming or at time of planting, according to individual instructions in Chapter Two.

Purchase and plant summer-flowering bulbs.

Mulch with organic matter.

Start a gardening watering schedule, watering soil thoroughly yet infrequently as a conservation measure. To check if soil needs to be watered, see if it feels dry 3 to 4 inches (7.5 to 10 cm.) down.

Bring spring bulb bouquets indoors.

After bulbs have bloomed, remove spent flowers but allow the leaves to develop, then disintegrate naturally.

If you wish, dig and store spring-blooming bulbs after the leaves start to die down.

SUMMER:

Continue weeding, watering, and deadheading.

Purchase and plant fall-blooming bulbs, such as autumn crocus.

Bring summer bulb bouquets indoors.

FALL:

Purchase and plant spring-flowering bulbs (September–October in Northern climates; November until early December in the South).

Bring autumn bulb bouquets indoors.

Divide bulbs after blooming according to individual instructions in Chapter Two.

Dig and store summer-flowering bulbs before frost.

Mulch to protect garden beds from cold temperatures and lock in soil nutrients over the winter.

WINTER:

Force spring bulbs indoors, using a refrigerator, cool basement, or cold frame for chilling.

Purchase and store summer-flowering bulbs.

Chapter Two
The 100 Best Bulbs
for Your Garden

DICENTRA	46	Squirrel Corn (D. Canadensis); Dutchman's-Breeches (D. Cucullaria); Turkey Corn (D. Eximia)
DIETES	47	African Iris
ERANTHIS	47	Winter Aconite
EREMURUS	48	Desert Candle; Foxtail Lily
ERYTHRONIUM	49	Dogtooth Violet; Trout Lily
EUCHARIS	50	Amazon Lily; Eucharist Lily
EUCOMIS	51	Pineapple Lily
EUCROSIA	52	Eucrosia
FREESIA	53	Freesia
FRITILLARIA	54	Crown Imperial; Checkered Lily
GALANTHUS	55	Snowdrop
GALTONIA	55	Summer Hyacinth
GLADIOLUS	56	Corn Flag; Sword Lily
GLOBBA	57	Dancing Lady Ginger
GLORIOSA	57	Climbing Lily
GLOXINIA	58	True Gloxinia
HABRANTHUS	59	Rain Lily
HAEMANTHUS	60	White Paintbrush
HEDYCHIUM	60	Butterfly Ginger
HELICONIA	61	Lobster Claws
HIPPEASTRUM	62	Florists' Amaryllis; Dutch Amaryllis
HYACINTHOIDES	63	English Bluebell; Spanish Bluebell
HYACINTHUS	64	Hyacinth
HYMENOCALLIS	65	Spider Lily
IPHEION	65	Spring Starflower
IPOMOEA	66	Sweet Potato Vine
IRIS	66	Dutch, German, Japanese, and Louisiana Irises
KAEMPFERIA	67	Peacock Ginger
KNIPHOFIA	68	Tritoma; Torch Lily; Red-hot Poker
KOHLERIA	69	Isoloma; Tree Gloxinia
LACHENALIA	70	Cape Cowslip
LEDEBOURIA	71	Silver Squill
LEUCOJUM	71	Snowflake
LILIUM	72	Lily
LYCORIS	73	Naked Lady; Hurricane Lily

MUSCARI	74	Grape Hyacinth
NARCISSUS	75	Daffodil; Telephone Flower
NEOMARICA	76	Walking Iris; Twelve Apostles
NERINE	77	Guernsey Lily
ORNITHOGALUM	77	Chincherinchee; Star-of-Bethlehem
OXALIS	78	Lucky Clover; Wood Sorrel
PANCRATIUM	79	Sea Daffodil
PLEIONE	80	Indian Crocus
POLIANTHES	81	Mexican Tuberose
PUSCHKINIA	82	Striped Squill
RANUNCULUS	83	Buttercup
RHODOHYPOXIS	83	Red Star
SCADOXUS	84	Blood Lily
SCHIZOSTYLIS	85	Crimson Flag; River Lily
SCILLA	86	Squill
SEEMANNIA	86	Seemannia
SINNINGIA	87	Florists' Gloxinia
SMITHIANTHA	88	Temple Bells
SPARAXIS	89	Wandflower; Velvet Flower
SPREKELIA	90	Jacobean Lily; Aztec Lily
STERNBERGIA	91	Winter Daffodil; Lily of the Field
TACCA	91	Batflower
TIGRIDIA	92	Mexican Shellflower
TRITONIA	93	Montbretia; Flame Freesia
TROPAEOLUM	93	Tuber Nasturtiums
TULBAGHIA	94	Society Garlic
TULIPA	95	Tulip
VALLOTA	96	Scarborough Lily
VELTHEIMIA	96	Forest Lily
ZANTEDESCHIA	97	Calla Lily
ZEPHYRANTHES	98	Rain Lily
ZINGIBER	99	Ginger

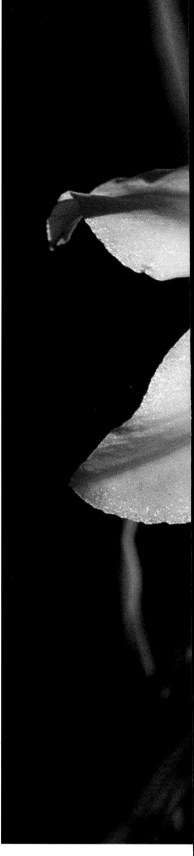

ACHIMENES
(ah-KIM-uh-neez)

Nut Orchid;
Hot-water Plant

GESNERIACEAE; gesneriad family

Height/habit: Bushy, upright to semicascading, 1 ft. (30 cm.) mounds.

Leaves: Simple; ovate, linear, or lanceolate, 1–2 in. (2.5–5 cm.) long, hairy; often olive above, flushed burgundy below.

Flowers: 5-lobed, tubular to funnelform, 1–2 in. (2.5–5 cm.) across, occasionally double; most colors, often with contrasting veins.

Season: Summer until fall, primarily through the longest days.

When to plant: Set scaly rhizomes 1 in. (2.5 cm.) deep, the same distance apart, in starting pots or where they are to grow, late winter through spring,

only in warm temperatures (60–80°F [15–26°C]). Despite love of warmth, often proves ground-hardy zone 9 and warmer.

Light: Sunny to half-sunny in spring, more shade in summer.

Soil: Humusy, well drained, moist.

Fertilizer: Alternate 30-10-10 and 15-30-15.

Storage: Store scaly rhizomes barely damp to nearly dry in barely damp to nearly dry peat moss or vermiculite, late fall to early spring, at 50–60°F (10–15°C).

Propagation: By natural increase of scaly rhizomes; or sow seeds in spring or individual scales as "seeds" in warm nursery conditions.

Uses: Beds, borders, pots, hanging baskets.

Fragrant Gladiolus

IRIDACEAE; iris family

Height/habit: Upright, 12–30 in. (30–76 cm.).

Leaves: Linear, to 1 ft. (30 cm.) long, resembling those of gladiolus.

Flowers: Loose spikes of 2–12, each to 3 in. (7.5 cm.) across; fragrant; white with reddish brown basal blotch.

Season: Late summer through early fall.

When to plant: Set corms 2–4 in. (5–10 cm.) deep, 4–8 in. (10–20 cm.) apart where they are to grow in spring, when weather is warm. Ground-hardy zone 9 and warmer.

Light: Sun a half day or more.

Soil: Well drained, moist.

Fertilizer: 5-10-5.

Storage: Store corms and cormels formed at their base in nearly dry peat moss or vermiculite, from late fall to spring, at 50–60°F (10–15°C).

Propagation: Remove and plant cormels in spring.

Uses: Beds, borders, pots, cut flowers.

AGAPANTHUS
(ag-ah-PANTH-us)
Lily of the Nile
AMARYLLIDACEAE; amaryllis family

Height/habit: Grasslike clumps, upright fountain form, 1–3 ft. (30–90 cm.) high/wide.

Leaves: Narrow or strap-shaped, up to 2 in. (5 cm.) across, 6–24 in. (15–61 cm.) long, rising in 2 ranks from a rhizome having fleshy roots.

Flowers: Umbels vary in number from a few to over 100, appearing atop a wiry to stiff scape, 1–4 ft. (30–122 cm.) long; blue or white.

Season: Spring through summer.

When to plant: Set transplants when available, ideally established in a container; roots recover slowly if disturbed. Grow outdoors all year zone 9 and warmer. In colder regions maintain indoors when frost threatens.

Light: Sun half day or more.

Soil: Well drained; moist spring through summer, dry side fall through winter.

Fertilizer: 5-10-5.

Storage: Avoid freezing; keep in sunny place but avoid severe drying; add water sparingly as needed to prevent large numbers of leaves from dying.

Propagation: Divide in late winter or spring from a clump having several sets of leaves. Fresh seeds grow readily, reaching flowering size in 3–5 years.

Uses: Beds, borders in frost-free climates, pots, cut flowers.

ALBUCA
(al-BEW-kah)

Sentry-in-the-box

LILIACEAE; lily family

Height/habit: Basal rosette of several leaves, 1–2 ft. (30–61 cm.).

Leaves: Concave at the base, to cylindrical or flat, to 1 ft. (30 cm.) long, arising from the bulb.

Flowers: Racemelike spikes, to 2.5 ft. (76 cm.) high, each 1–2 in. (2.5–5 cm.) across; white or pale yellow with pronounced green striping on the outside; fragrant.

Season: Spring through early summer. Foliage disappears around midsummer.

When to plant: Set bulbs 2–4 in. (5–10 cm.) deep, 9–12 in. (22.5–30 cm.) apart in fall or when dormant.

Light: Sun half day or more.

Soil: Well drained; moist spring until flowers finish, gradually drying off.

Fertilizer: 5-10-5.

Storage: Only to protect from freezing in winter at 50–60°F (10–15°C) until planting time.

Propagation: Remove offsets at planting time; seedlings bloom in 3–4 years.

Uses: Beds, borders zones 9–10 and warmer, pots all climates.

ALLIUM
(AL-lee-um)

Ornamental Onion

LILIACEAE; lily family

Height/habit: Grassy to onionlike clumps, 8–24 in. (20–61 cm.).

Leaves: Straplike and hollow, either flat or round, growing to 1 ft. (30 cm.) long.

Flowers: Loose or tightly packed heads, 1–6 in. (2.5–15 cm.) across on bare stalks above the leaves; lilac purple, yellow, white, pink, or blue.

Season: Spring through summer, depending on the variety.

When to plant: Set bulbs or transplants where they are to grow in spring or fall, or when available. Most are perennial all zones.

Light: Sun half day or more.

Soil: Well drained, moist to on the dry side.

Fertilizer: 5-10-5.

Storage: Store dormant bulbs in dry, dark, frost-free place, at 50–60°F (10–15°C) in peat moss or vermiculite, in winter until planting time.

Propagation: Divide clumps spring or fall. Seedlings bloom in 3 years.

Uses: Beds, borders, pots, cutting, drying. Leaves of *A. schoenoprasum* are the edible herb chives.

ALPINIA
(al-PINE-ee-ah)
Shell Ginger
ZINGIBERACEAE; ginger family

Height/habit: Erect clumps 5–10 ft. (1.5–3 m.) high/wide.

Leaves: Appear all along the stalks, each 1–2 ft. (30–61 cm.) long, to 5 in. (12.5 cm.) wide.

Flowers: Bell-shaped in dense clusters to 1 ft. (30 cm.) long; fragrant; white or flushed pink with red and brown details.

Season: Summer.

When to plant: Set transplants when available, ideally spring after the weather is warm and settled. Best for ground planting zone 10 and warmer; roots may survive light frost but recovery to flowering may be slow. Remove canes annually, after they have flowered.

Light: Part sun to part shade.

Soil: Humusy, well drained, generous moisture in summer.

Fertilizer: 5-10-5.

Storage: Only to prevent freezing; in winter in dry peat moss or vermiculite; avoid temperatures below 60°F (15°C).

Propagation: Divide rhizomatous roots in spring.

Uses: Beds, backgrounds, accents, large containers.

ALSTROEMERIA
(al-stroh-MEER-ee-ah)
Peruvian Lily

ALSTROEMERIACEAE;
alstroemeria family

Height/habit: Upright,
1.5–2.5 ft. (45–76 cm.), forming
clumps or colonizing.

Leaves: Linear to lanceolate,
1–5 in. (2.5–12.5 cm.) long,
growing from the base and
all along the stems; whorled
in *A. psittacina*.

Flowers: 1–3 in. (2.5–7.5 cm.)
across in terminal clusters,
resembling the Dutch amaryllis
blossom in miniature; in
A. caryophyllaea, fragrant yellow, orange, or white with red
tips; in *A. psittacina*, dark red
tipped green with brown spots.

Season: Midwinter through
early summer, depending on
the species and climate.

When to plant: Set transplants
when available. Tends to be
dormant in hottest weather,
grows mostly in cooler seasons. *A. pulchella* hardy zone 5
and warmer, with protection
in coldest sections. Seeds
started in a cool greenhouse in
the fall flower after 2–3 seasons.

Light: Sun half day or more.

Soil: Well drained; evenly
moist while in active growth
(cool seasons), drier in summer. Cool (around 50°F
[10°C]) soil in fall and early
winter helps set buds.

Fertilizer: 5-10-5.

Storage: Rest bulbs from
receipt until planting time in
peat moss or vermiculite at
50–60°F (10–15°C).

Propagation: Sow seeds in
summer; divide in spring.

Uses: Beds, borders, pots,
long-lasting cut flower.
A. psittacina can be a useful
(at times striking, on occasion
invasive) ground cover zone 9
and warmer.

AMARYLLIS
(am-ah-RILL-iss)
Belladonna Lily
AMARYLLIDACEAE; amaryllis
family

Height/habit: Upright, self-reliant clumps of leaves fall-winter, 2–3 ft. (60–90 cm.) tall/wide.

Leaves: Straplike, to 18 in. (45 cm.) long.

Flowers: In an umbel atop a naked, reddish scape, 15–30 in. (35–75 cm.) tall, each 3–4 in. (8–10 cm.) long/wide; rose-red to pale pink or near white.

Season: Late summer-early fall.

When to plant: Set the bulb early fall, immediately after flowering, with neck at soil surface. Cold hardy zone 8 and warmer, zone 7 if protected.

Light: Sunny to half-sunny.

Soil: Humus-rich, well-drained, moist except on the dry side late spring-early summer.

Fertilizer: 5-10-5.

Uses: Beds, borders, large pots, cutting.

ANEMONE
(ah·NEM·oh·nee)

Windflower

RANUNCULACEAE; buttercup
family

Height/habit: *A. blanda*
types 6–8 in. (15–20 cm.).
A. coronaria varieties form
a basal rosette of foliage
resembling parsley, then
flower on straight stems to
1.5 ft. (45 cm.).
Leaves: Basal, much divided,
1–3 in. (2.5–7.5 cm.) across.
Flowers: Daisylike in
A. blanda, 1–2 in. (2.5–5 cm.)
across. Poppylike in
A. coronaria, 2–3 in. (5–7.5 cm.)
across; white, blue, pink, red,
or rose.
Season: Winter through
spring. *A. coronaria* grows
well outdoors in mild climates.
When to plant: Set tuberous
rhizomes 1–2 in. (2.5–5 cm.)
deep, 6–12 in. (15–30 cm.)
apart in fall. Zone 7 and colder
set *A. coronaria* in spring for
blooms in summer.
Light: Sunny to partly sunny;
more shade for *A. blanda*.
Soil: Humusy, well drained,
moist while in active growth.
Fertilizer: 5-10-5.
Storage: Store dormant
rhizomes from receipt until
planting time in peat moss or
vermiculite in a dry and dark
place with moderate temperatures (50–70°F [10–21°C]).
Propagation: Sow seeds in late
summer or early fall.
Uses: *A. blanda* types carpet
ground, often interplanted
with tulips, hyacinths, and
daffodils; cut flowers.

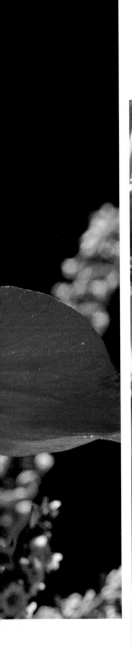

ANIGOZANTHOS
(ah-nee-go-ZANTH-oss)

Kangaroo Paw

HAEMODORACEAE; bloodwort
family

Height/habit: Clumps with
flowering stalks rising 3–5 ft.
(1–1.5 m.).

Leaves: Linear or sword-
shaped, 1–1.5 ft. (30–45 cm.)
long.

Flowers: 1-sided spikes, woolly,
1–3 in. (2.5–7.5 cm.) long; red
to yellow to greenish; showy
in bloom, unusual.

Season: Late spring through
fall; periodically cut back
bloomed-out spikes to the
ground.

When to plant: Set rootstocks
with growth eyes at ground
level in spring or early fall;
set transplants when available.
Winter-hardy zone 9 and
warmer.

Light: Sun half day or more.

Soil: Well drained, moist;
maintain on the dry side in
winter.

Fertilizer: 5-10-5.

Storage: Store rootstocks out
of the ground in dry peat moss
and moderate temperatures
(50–60°F [10–15°C]), as briefly
as possible, from receipt until
planting time.

Propagation: Divide established clumps in spring or
early fall.

Uses: Beds, borders, large
containers, cut flowers.

ARISAEMA
(air-iss-EE-mah)

Jack-in-the-pulpit

ARACEAE; aroid family

Height/habit: Erect, 1–2 ft. (30–61 cm.).

Leaves: 1–3 per tuber, divided, 3–5-parted, 9–12 in. (22.5–30 cm.) long.

Flowers: Clublike spadix surrounded by an ornamental spathe; combinations of green, white, and purple-brown.

Season: Late spring through early summer. Leaves attractive in summer; red berries in fall.

When to plant: Set tubers 4–6 in. (10–15 cm.) deep, 1 ft. (30 cm.) apart in fall or early spring. Set transplants when available. North American arisaemas and some from Asia are winter-hardy to zone 5; those from milder climates require wintering in a frost-free place.

Light: Part sun to part shade.

Soil: Humusy, well drained, moist.

Fertilizer: 5-10-5.

Storage: Rest tubers as necessary in dry peat moss, with moderate temperatures (50–60°F [10–15°C]) and darkness until planting time.

Propagation: Remove offsets at transplanting time or sow seeds in spring.

Uses: Beds, borders, wild gardens.

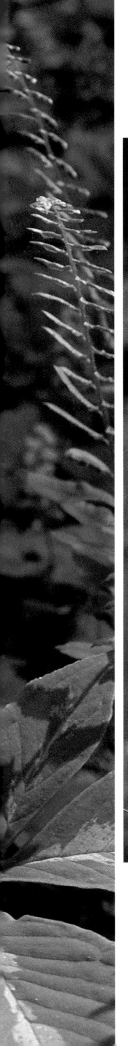

ASPHODELINE
(ass-foh-del-LYE-nee)
Asphodel
LILIACEAE; lily family

Height/habit: Grasslike
clumps, 1–1.5 ft. (30–45 cm.)
high/wide. Dormant in winter.
Leaves: Linear, to 1 ft. (30 cm.)
long.
Flowers: Starry, 1–2 in.
(2.5–5 cm.) across, in dense,
cylindrical racemes, to 2 ft.
(61 cm.) high; yellow; fragrant.
Season: Early to midsummer.
When to plant: Set clumps of
thickened roots with growth
eyes 1–2 in. (2.5–5 cm.) deep,
6–8 in. (15–20 cm.) apart in
early spring or fall. Set transplants when available.
Ground-hardy zone 5 and
warmer.
Light: Sun half day or more.
Soil: Well drained, moist.
Fertilizer: 5-10-5.
Storage: Store root clumps in
dry peat moss, darkness, and
moderate temperatures
(50–60°F [10–15°C]) from
receipt until planting time.
Propagation: Divide at transplanting time or sow seeds in
fall or spring.
Uses: Beds, borders, cut
flowers.

ASPHODELUS
(ass-FOD-el-us)

Silver Rod

LILIACEAE; lily family

Height/habit: Erect, 2–5 ft. (61–150 cm.).

Leaves: Coarse, grasslike, in clumps, 1–1.5 ft. (30–45 cm.) high/wide. Dormant in winter.

Flowers: Starry, 1–2 in. (2.5–5 cm.) across, in showy, erect spikes 1.5–5 ft. (45–150 cm.) high; white or pink.

Season: Late spring through early summer.

When to plant: Set clumps of thickened roots with the growth eyes 1–2 in. (2.5–5 cm.) deep, 6–8 in. (15–20 cm.) apart in early spring or fall. Set transplants when available. Ground-hardy zones 6–7 and warmer.

Light: Sun half day or more.

Soil: Well drained, moist.

Fertilizer: 5-10-5.

Storage: Store root clumps in dry peat moss, darkness, and moderate temperatures (50–60°F [10–15°C]) from receipt until planting time.

Propagation: Divide at transplanting time or sow seeds in fall or spring.

Uses: Beds, borders, cut flowers.

BEGONIA
(be-GOH-nee-ah)

Tuberous Begonia

BEGONIACEAE; begonia family

Height/habit: *Begonia* x *tuberhybrida* upright or cascading, 1–3 ft. (30–90 cm.).

Leaves: Lightly hairy, angel-wing-shaped, 5 in. (12.5 cm.) long x 3 in. (7.5 cm.) wide; bright green; stalks and stems often flushed reddish copper.

Flowers: Single or double, 2–8 in. (5–20 cm.) across, in a variety of forms, including camellia, rose, carnation, and picotee; most colors except blue.

Season: Summer until early fall. They bloom while days are longest and are not suited to gardens where temperatures rise above 80°F (26°C).

When to plant: Set tubers to root in pots or flats indoors 8–12 weeks before planting-out weather. Upright varieties can be set in beds; most tuberous begonias are grown in containers.

Light: Half sun to half shade; the cooler the temperatures, the more sun they need.

Soil: Humusy, well drained, moist throughout the growing season, dry while dormant.

Fertilizer: 5-10-5.

Storage: Store tubers in nearly dry peat moss and moderate temperatures (50–60°F [10–15°C]) from fall until planting time the next late winter through spring.

Propagation: Sow seeds winter through spring in a warm, moist, bright place; divide tubers, each part with a growth eye, at planting time.

Uses: Beds, borders, pots, hanging baskets.

BEGONIA

(be-GOH-nee-ah)

Hardy Begonia

BEGONIACEAE; begonia family

Height/habit: *B. grandis* upright, 1.5–2.5 ft. (45–76 cm.) high/wide.

Leaves: Angel-wing-shaped, 5 in. (12.5 cm.) long x 3 in. (7.5 cm.) wide; olive above, flushed red below.

Flowers: 1 in. (2.5 cm.) across in drooping cymes; fragrant; pink (white in 'Alba').

Season: Midsummer to fall.

When to plant: Set bulblets 1 in. (2.5 cm.) deep, 8–12 in. (20–30 cm.) apart in spring. Bulblets form annually in the leaf axils. Ground-hardy zone 7 and warmer.

Light: Half sun to half shade.

Soil: Humusy, well drained, moist.

Fertilizer: 5-10-5.

Storage: Place bulblets in dry peat moss, darkness, and moderate temperatures (50–60°F [10–15°C]) during winter until planting time.

Propagation: In spring, plant bulblets formed the previous growing season.

Uses: Beds, borders, ground cover.

BLETILLA

(bleh-TILL-ah)

Chinese Ground Orchid

ORCHIDACEAE; orchid family

Height/habit: Upright, forming good-sized clumps, 8–20 in. (20–50 cm.) high/wide.

Leaves: Narrow, arching, pleated, palmlike, 8–12 in. (20–30 cm.) long.

Flowers: Racemes of 3–12 rise above the leaves, each 1–2 in. (2.5–5 cm.) across; purple or white.

Season: Early to midsummer.

When to plant: Set tuberlike roots 1–2 in. (2.5–5 cm.) deep 6–8 in. (15–20 cm.) apart in fall or early spring. Set transplants when available. Do not disturb unnecessarily; established, crowded clumps bloom best. Ground-hardy zone 8 and warmer.

Light: Half sun to half shade.

Soil: Humusy, well drained, moist while in active growth.

Fertilizer: 5-10-5.

Storage: Store roots briefly in dry peat moss and moderate temperatures (50–60°F [10–15°C]) from receipt until planting time.

Propagation: Divide rootstocks in fall or early spring.

Uses: Beds, borders, wild gardens, pots.

CALADIUM
(kal-LAY-dee-um)

Fancy-leaved Caladium

ARACEAE; aroid family

Height/habit: Upright, rounded clumps, 1–3 ft. (30–90 cm.) high/wide.
Leaves: Arrowhead-shaped, 2–12 in. (5–30 cm.) long by half to two-thirds as wide; lance-leaved cultivars thrive in sun. Leaves typically veined, speckled, or banded with a contrasting color.

Flowers: Mostly hidden by leaves; resemble the calla lily; gardeners usually remove them as soon as the buds appear in order to produce beautiful foliage.
Season: Spring and summer.
When to plant: Set caladium tubers 2–4 in. (5–10 cm.) deep, 6–12 in. (15–30 cm.) apart when soil is warm in spring; tubers can be started indoors in separate pots 8–12 weeks before planting-out weather; sometimes proves ground-hardy zone 9 and warmer.
Light: Sun for lance-leaved cultivars; equal amounts sun and shade for standard large, arrowhead varieties.

Soil: Humusy, well drained, moist while in active growth.
Fertilizer: 5-10-5.
Storage: Store tubers in dry peat moss or vermiculite at 50–60°F (10–15°C) from receipt until planting time.
Propagation: Remove offsets from tubers in spring.
Uses: Beds, borders, pots.

CAMASSIA
(kah-MASS-ee-ah)

Camass; Wild Hyacinth

LILIACEAE; lily family

Height/habit: Upright clumps, 1–1.5 ft. (30–45 cm.) high/wide.
Leaves: Grassy, narrow, tapering, 1–3 ft. (30–90 cm.) long.
Flowers: Dense spikes rising from center of plant; starry, 1–2 in. (2.5–5 cm.) across; blue, white, purple, or cream.
Season: Late spring.
When to plant: Set bulbs 4 in. (10 cm.) deep, 9 in. (22.5 cm.) apart in fall. Ground-hardy zone 5 and warmer.
Light: Sun half day or more.

Soil: Well drained, moist; keep dry during summer resting period.
Fertilizer: 5-10-5.
Storage: Store bulbs in dry peat moss at 50–60°F (10–15°C) until planting time.
Propagation: Divide crowded clumps in fall.
Uses: Beds, borders, cut flowers, perimeter plantings for pond and bog gardens.

CANNA
(KAN-nah)

Indian Shot

CANNACEAE; canna family

Height/habit: Upright clumps, 4–12 ft. (1.2–3.6 m.) high by half as wide.

Leaves: Reminiscent of those of banana; simple, rounded, entire; 1–4 ft. (30–122 cm.) long by about half as wide; often with fine edging of red-brown. In *Canna* x *generalis* 'Striata' the red-margined bright green leaves are feathered and striped with cream yellow.

Flowers: Terminal clusters resembling butterfly ginger but larger; most colors except blue and purple.

Season: Summer in cold climates, spring through fall zone 8 and warmer. Prompt removal of spent flowers increases bloom and enhances appearance. After all the flowers on a stalk have bloomed, it can be cut back to the ground.

When to plant: Set tuberlike rhizomes 5 in. (12.5 cm.) deep, 10 in. (25 cm.) apart when soil is warm in spring. Set transplants when available. Ground-hardy zone 7 and warmer.

Light: Sun half day or more.

Soil: Humusy, well drained, moist during active growing season; pots of cannas can be left standing in saucers of water.

Fertilizer: 5-10-5.

Storage: Store tuberlike rhizomes in dry peat moss at 50–60°F (10–15°C) from light frost season in fall to spring planting.

Propagation: Divide rhizomes in spring or sow seeds indoors 12–16 weeks before warm weather.

Uses: Beds, borders, large pots, perimeter plantings for ponds and bog gardens.

CHASMANTHE
(chaz-MANTH-ee)

Pennants

IRIDACEAE; iris family

Height/habit: Upright clumps, 2–4 ft. (61–122 cm.) high/wide.
Leaves: 1–2 in. (2.5–5 cm.) wide, 1–2 ft. (30–61 cm.) long.
Flowers: Erect spikes growing above the leaves, to 2 in. (5 cm.) long; orange-red with yellow or green.
Season: Spring through early summer.
When to plant: Set the corms 2–4 in. (5–10 cm.) deep, 4–8 in. (10–20 cm.) apart, fall zone 8 and warmer, spring zone 7 and colder.
Light: Sun half day or more.
Soil: Well drained, moist while in active growth.
Fertilizer: 5-10-5.
Storage: Store corms in dry peat moss at 50–60°F (10–15°C) from receipt until planting time.
Propagation: Divide established clumps in spring.
Uses: Beds, borders, pots, cut flowers.

CHIONODOXA
(key-on-oh-DOX-ah)

Glory-of-the-snow

LILIACEAE; lily family

Height/habit: Grassy clumps, 6–8 in. (15–20 cm.) high/wide.
Leaves: Narrow, to 6 in. (15 cm.) long.
Flowers: 4–6 per terminal raceme, each to 1 in. (2.5 cm.) across; blue, white, or pink.
Season: Early spring.
When to plant: Set bulbs 3 in. (7.5 cm.) deep, 2 in. (5 cm.) apart in fall. Ground-hardy zone 5 and warmer.

Light: Sun in spring, shade acceptable at other times.
Soil: Well drained; moist fall through spring, keep on the dry side in summer.
Fertilizer: 5-10-5.
Storage: Store bulbs in dry peat moss at 50–60°F (10–15°C) from receipt until planting time.
Propagation: Divide established clumps in fall.
Uses: Beds, borders, pots; excellent for planting under deciduous trees and shrubs since they do not leaf out until the chionodoxa leaves have done their season's gathering of solar energy.

CLIVIA
(KLYE-vee-ah)
Kaffir Lily
AMARYLLIDACEAE; amaryllis family

Height/habit: Upright, evergreen clumps, 1–2 ft. (30–61 cm.) high/wide.

Leaves: Strap-shaped, 2–3 in. (5–7.5 cm.) wide, 1–1.5 ft. (30–45 cm.) long.

Flowers: Many-flowered umbels atop stiff stalks; each flower to 2 in. (5 cm.) across; apricot, orange, scarlet, rarely yellow.

Season: Winter through spring, depending on climate and treatment. Suited to ground planting zone 10 and warmer.

When to plant: Best to pur chase transplants in bloom so you know the color and form are superior.

Light: Half sun to half shade.

Soil: Humusy, well drained; moist, except keep on the dry side in fall and winter.

Fertilizer: 5-10-5.

Storage: Store potted plant in cool (40–60°F [4–15°C]) but not freezing temperatures; keep on the dry side in fall and early winter, but do not let leaves die.

Propagation: Remove offsets in spring or sow seeds as soon as they are ripe. Set each young plant in a 5-in. (12-5 cm.) clay pot and do not transplant to a larger size until it has bloomed, usually within 3 years.

Uses: Pots and cut flowers in all climates; beds zone 10 and warmer.

COLCHICUM
(KOLE-chick-um)

Autumn Crocus

LILIACEAE; lily family

Height/habit: Clumps of spring foliage, to 1 ft. (30 cm.) high/wide.

Leaves: Basal, to 3 in. (7.5 cm.) wide x 1 ft. (30 cm.) long.

Flowers: Clusters, each to 6 in. (15 cm.) across by 10 in. (25 cm.) high; white, purple, or pink; double in 'Waterlily.'

Season: Fall.

When to plant: Set bulbs 2–3 in. (5–7.5 cm.) deep, 4–6 in. (10–15 cm.) apart in late summer or early fall. Ground-hardy zone 6 and warmer.

Light: Sun half day or more.

Soil: Well drained, moist spring and fall; during summer dormancy, keep on the dry side.

Fertilizer: 5-10-5.

Storage: Store in dry peat moss at 50–60°F (10–15°C), as briefly as possible, from receipt until planting time.

Propagation: Separate corms at planting time or sow seeds.

Uses: Beds, borders, pots.

COLOCASIA
(koh-low-KAY-see-ah)

Elephant's Ear; Taro

ARACEAE; aroid family

Height/habit: Upright stalks arising directly from the tuber, to 5 ft. (1.5 m.) high/wide.

Leaves: Arrowhead- or shield-shaped, to 3 ft. (1 m.) long by half as wide; prominent veins and satin texture.

Flowers: Calla-type spathe hidden by much taller leaf stalks; pale yellow.

Season: Late spring through summer.

When to plant: Set tubers 4–6 in. (10–15 cm.) deep, 1–1.5 ft. (30–45 cm.) apart when the soil is warm. Ground-hardy zone 8 and warmer.

Light: Half sun to half shade.

Soil: Humusy, well drained; moist during the active growing season.

Fertilizer: 20-20-20 or 5-10-5.

Storage: Rest tubers in dry peat moss at 50–60°F (10–15°C) from fall through winter.

Propagation: Remove offsets from tubers at planting time.

Uses: Beds, borders, pots, accent plants.

CONVALLARIA
(kon-val-LAY-ree-ah)

Lily of the Valley

LILIACEAE; lily family

Height/habit: Dense carpets, to
8 in. (20 cm.), with indefinite
diameter.

Leaves: Lanceolate to ovate to
elliptic, to 8 in. (20 cm.) long
x 2 in. (5 cm.) wide.

Flowers: Very small to .5 in.
(1.25 cm.), fragrant nodding
bells on a 1-sided raceme,
growing among or slightly
above the leaves in single or
double forms; white or pink.

Season: Late spring through
early summer.

When to plant: Set pips
(upright rootstock) 1–2 in.
(2.5–5 cm.) deep, 6 in. (15 cm.)
apart in fall or early spring.
Set transplants when available.
Divide crowded stands after
a few years. Cold-hardy almost
everywhere but languishes
zone 9 and warmer. Pips potted in fall and subjected to cold
temperatures (minor freezing)
8–12 weeks can then be forced
into early bloom in a window
garden.

Light: Half sun to half shade.

Soil: Humusy, well drained,
moist.

Fertilizer: 20-20-20 or 5-10-5.

Storage: Store pips in barely
damp peat moss at 40–50°F
(4–10°C) from fall through
winter until planting time.

Propagation: Divide crowded
clumps early spring or fall.

Uses: Beds, borders, rock
gardens, ground cover,
cut flowers.

CORYDALIS
(koh-RID-ah-liss)

Fumaria

FUMARIACEAE; fumitory family

Height/habit: Upright rosettes, 9–12 in. (22.5–30 cm.) high/wide.

Leaves: Fernlike, 6–12 in. (15–30 cm.) long.

Flowers: Resemble bleeding heart (*Dicentra*), though smaller, in erect racemes of 10–20; rose, purple, pink, white, or yellow.

Season: Early spring through summer. Resilient yellow *C. lutea* blooms constantly from late spring until end of summer.

When to plant: Set root divisions in early spring or fall, growth eyes near soil surface, 6 in. (15 cm.) apart. Grows best zones 5–7. Established plantings self-sow generously.

Light: Half sun to half shade.

Soil: Humusy, well drained, moist.

Fertilizer: 5-10-5.

Storage: Store rootstocks in barely damp peat moss at 40–60°F (4–15°C), as briefly as possible, from receipt until planting time.

Propagation: Divide rootstock clumps in fall or early spring; alternatively, sow seeds or transplant self-sown seedlings.

Uses: Beds, borders, rock or wild gardens, pockets in rock walls.

CRINUM
(KRYE-num)

Florida Swamp Lily; Milk-and-wine Lily

AMARYLLIDACEAE; amaryllis family

Height/habit: Bold, upright, 3–6 ft. (1–1.8 m.) high/wide.

Leaves: Strap- or sword-shaped, to 3 ft. (1 m.) long, arranged in a spiral.

Flowers: Funnelform or spidery, each 3–5 in. (7.5–12.5 cm.) across, a few to many atop a stiff scape, 2–3 ft. (61–90 cm.) high; white, pink, rose, or red and white.

Season: Spring through summer.

When to plant: Set bulbs up to their necks, 1 ft. (30 cm.) apart in spring or fall; set transplants when available. Ground-hardy zones 8–9 and warmer. Favored landscape plant in Florida, along the Gulf Coast and in Southern California.

Light: Sun half day or more.

Soil: Humusy, well drained, moist.

Fertilizer: 20-20-20 or 5-10-5.

Storage: Store bulbs briefly in dry peat moss at 50–60°F (10–15°C) from receipt until planting time.

Propagation: Remove offsets in spring or fall or sow seeds (first flowers in 3–4 seasons).

Uses: Beds, borders, large pots, cut flowers, accent plant; surrounding pond or bog gardens.

CROCOSMIA
(kroh-KAZH-mee-ah)

Copper Tip;
Montbretia

IRIDACEAE; iris family

Height/habit: Upright grassy clumps, 2–4 ft. (61–122 cm.) high/wide.

Leaves: Sword-shaped, pleated, resembling those of gladiolus; clustered mostly toward the base, 1–2 ft. (30–61 cm.) long.

Flowers: Borne on wiry, graceful stems standing above the leaves, gracefully curving so that the individual flowers, to 2 in. (5 cm.) across, all face same direction; orange-red or yellow. Cultivar 'Lucifer' is said to have hybrid vigor and will form a remarkable colony in a few years.

Season: Summer.

When to plant: Set corms 2 in. (5 cm.) deep, 6 in. (15 cm.) apart in spring or fall. Set transplants when available. Ground-hardy zone 7 and warmer; in colder regions, apply mulch or other protection.

Light: Full sun to half sun (more shade where summers are hot).

Soil: Well drained, moist.

Fertilizer: 5-10-5.

Storage: Store corms in dry peat moss at 50–60°F (10–15°C) from receipt until planting time.

Propagation: Divide corms in spring or fall or sow seeds in spring.

Uses: Beds, borders, naturalizing, pots, long-lasting cut flower, hummingbird attractant.

CROCUS
(KROH-kuss)

Crocus

IRIDACEAE; iris family

Height/habit: Grassy, 6–12 in. (15–30 cm.).

Leaves: Narrow and linear 4–12 in. (10–30 cm.) long, with a prominent silvery midrib accompanying those that bloom in spring but preceding fall bloomers.

Flowers: Goblets 1–3 in. (2.5–7.5 cm.) across, rising directly from corms; some fragrant; yellow, white, cream, blue, or striped.

Season: Fall (*C. asturicus*, *C. cancellatus*, *C. kotschyanus*, *C. laevigatus*, *C. longiflorus*, *C. ochroleucus*, *C. pulchellus*, *C. sativus*, *C. speciosus*); winter through early spring (many species and the large Dutch hybrids).

When to plant: Set corms 3–4 in. (7.5–10 cm.) deep and the same distance apart in late summer through early fall.

Ground-hardy as cold as zone 3 but might not persist in gardens warmer than zone 7. Winter and spring crocuses can be potted in the fall, set to root in a cold (40–50°F [4–10°C]) but not freezing place for 8–12 weeks, then brought inside for early bloom in a cool window.

Light: Sun half day or more.

Soil: Well drained; moist fall through spring and on the dry side in summer.

Fertilizer: 5-10-5.

Storage: Store corms in dry peat moss at 40–50°F (4–10°C) from receipt until planting time.

Propagation: Separate clumps having many corms in fall or sow seeds. Crocuses multiply on their own, eventually forming large colonies.

Uses: Beds, borders, rock gardens, naturalizing, pots.

CURCUMA
(kur-KEW-mah)
Hidden Ginger
ZINGIBERACEAE; ginger family

Height/habit: Tidy, upright clumps, 1.5–2.5 ft. (45–76 cm.) high and half as wide.

Leaves: Long stalks, 1–1.5 ft. (30–45 cm.) tall by one-third as wide.

Flowers: Terminal spike to 8 in. (20 cm.) long; pale yellow cupped bracts; *C. roscoeana* turns fiery orange-scarlet and persists several weeks.

Season: Summer through early fall.

When to plant: Set tubers 2 in. (5 cm.) deep, 6–12 in. (15–30 cm.) apart in warm soil in spring; set transplants when available. Ground-hardy zone 10 and warmer; outstanding for containers in any climate. Dies to ground fall through spring.

Light: Half sun to half shade.

Soil: Humusy, well drained; moist in summer but nearly dry while resting.

Fertilizer: 20-20-20 or 5-10-5.

Storage: Store tubers in dry peat moss at 50–60°F (10–15°C) during winter until planting time.

Propagation: Remove offsets at planting time in spring.

Uses: Beds, borders, pots.

CYCLAMEN
(SIKE-lah-men; SICK-lah-men)

Persian Violet; Florists' Cyclamen

PRIMULACEAE; primrose family

Height/habit: Mounds or rosettes, 4–10 in. (10–25 cm.) high/wide.

Leaves: Heart-, kidney-, or ivy-shaped on wiry stalks arising directly from the tuber, each 1–2 in. (2.5–5 cm.) across, often with contrasting veins or pronounced silver variegation on green.

Flowers: Inverted/reflexed, 1–3 in. (2.5–7.5 cm.) across; some with sweet fragrance; red, rose, pink, violet, purple, or white.

Season: Winter through spring. Regular and miniature forms of florists' cyclamen (*C. indicum*) tolerate cold to about 28°F (-2°C) and can be used zone 9 and warmer for color where impatiens bloom in warm weather. Other species are hardy zone 5 and warmer and bloom during winter mild spells or spring.

When to plant: Set transplants when available, usually spring, fall, or winter.

Light: Part sun to part shade.

Soil: Humusy, well drained; moist while in active growth, on the dry side at other times.

Fertilizer: 5-10-5 or 14-14-14.

Storage: Store florists' cyclamen tubers in their pots, nearly dry, in moderate temperatures (60–70°F [15–21°C]) late spring until late summer, when it is time to repot and activate growth for a new flowering season.

Propagation: Sow seeds from winter through spring for flowers in 12–18 months after planting.

Uses: Beds, borders, pots.

CYRTANTHUS
(sur-TANTH-us)

Miniature Amaryllis

AMARYLLIDACEAE; amaryllis family

Height/habit: Grassy clumps, 8–15 in. (20–38 cm.).
Leaves: Narrow, to 1 ft. (30 cm.) long.
Flowers: Nodding, fragrant clusters at the end of stems to 1 ft. (30 cm.) high, each a narrow funnel flaring at the apex into 6 petals; white, pink, yellow, or orange-red.
Season: Summer or winter, sometimes fall or spring.
When to plant: Set dormant bulbs with the tips at soil level 6–12 in. (15–30 cm.) apart in fall or spring; set transplants when available. Ground-hardy zone 9 and warmer.
Light: Sun half day or more.
Soil: Humusy, well drained; moist during active season, on the dry side while resting.
Fertilizer: 5-10-5 or 14-14-14.
Storage: Store bulbs in dry peat moss at 55–65°F (13–18°C) from receipt until planting time.
Propagation: Divide at planting time or sow seeds. Like many amaryllids this one does best if set in a fairly large pot and left undisturbed for several years. Many offsets will form and there will be an extraordinary number of flowers.
Uses: Beds, borders, pots, cut flowers.

DAHLIA
(DAL-ee-ah)
Common Dahlia
COMPOSITAE; daisy family

Height/habit: Bushy, upright (with staking), 4–8 ft. (1.2–2.4 m.) high and half as wide.

Leaves: Compound, dark green, in pairs along hollow, jointed, smooth stems 1–2 in. (2.5–5 cm.) long.

Flowers: Daisylike but in at least 15 recognized classes: single, mignon, orchid-flowering, anemone-flowering, collarette, duplex, peony-flowering, incurved cactus, recurved or straight cactus, semicactus, formal decorative, informal decorative, ball, miniature, and pompon; 1–12 in. (2.5–30 cm.) across; most colors except blue, often bicolored.

Season: Midsummer to fall frost.

When to plant: When weather is warm and settled in spring, set each tuber in planting hole 6 in. (15 cm.) deep, 2–3 ft. (61–90 cm.) apart; cover initially with 2–3 in. (5–7.5 cm.) soil; after growth commences, fill remainder of hole. Ground-hardy in warmer regions, but tubers multiply so rapidly that plants go into decline unless dug and divided every year or two. Best performance where summers are mildly hot and there is a protracted fall season with cool but not freezing temperatures.

Light: Sun half day or more.

Soil: Humusy, well drained; moist throughout the growing season.

Fertilizer: 5-10-5 or 14-14-14.

Storage: Rest tubers in dry peat moss at 50–60°F (10–15°C) from fall through spring.

Propagation: Divide clumps in spring; be sure that each tuber is separated with a portion of the neck and a growing eye.

Uses: Beds, borders, large containers, cut flowers.

DICENTRA
(deye-SENT-rah)

Squirrel Corn
(D. CANADENSIS)

Dutchman's-Breeches
(D. CUCULLARIA)

Turkey Corn
(D. EXIMIA)

Height/habit: Upright basal rosettes 1–2 ft. (30–61 cm.) high/wide.

Leaves: Compound, much cut, 10–18 in. (25–45 cm.) long/wide.

Flowers: Racemes of nodding, irregular, 1–2 in. (2.5–5 cm.) long, often 2-spurred at the base; greenish white or purple-tinged (*D. canadensis*), white with yellow tips (*D. cucullaria*), white or lavender pink to dark purplish red (*D. eximia*).

Season: Spring (*D. canadensis*, *D. cucullaria*); spring through summer (*D. eximia*).

When to plant: Set tubers or fleshy rhizomes in fall, 1–2 in. (2.5–5 cm.) deep; set transplants when available. Cold-hardy to zone 4 but not suited to zone 9 and warmer.

Light: Half sun to half shade.

Soil: Humusy, well drained, moist.

Fertilizer: 5-10-5 or 14-14-14.

Storage: Store in dry peat moss and moderate temperatures (50–70°F [10–21°C]) until planting time.

Propagation: Divide established clumps late summer through fall; also by self-sown seedlings.

Uses: Beds, borders, wild or rock gardens.

DIETES
(deye-EE-teez)

African Iris

IRIDACEAE; iris family

Height/habit: Grassy clumps to 2 ft. (61 cm.) high/wide.
Leaves: Linear to sword-shaped in 2 ranks, 2–2.5 ft. (61–76 cm.) long, evergreen.
Flowers: Hover like butterflies above the leaves, 2–4 in. (5–10 cm.) across; lemon yellow with dark brown basal spot (*D. bicolor*) or white with yellow or brown spots and blue markings (*D. vegeta*).
Season: Summer; old bloom stalks often flower again.
When to plant: Set transplants when available. Winter-hardy zone 9 and warmer. Elsewhere containerize and bring indoors during freezing weather.
Light: Full sun to half sun.
Soil: Well drained, moist.
Fertilizer: 5-10-5.
Storage: Store upright in barely damp peat moss, as briefly as possible, until planting time.
Propagation: Divide established clumps in fall or spring.
Uses: Beds, borders, pots.

ERANTHIS
(ee-RANTH-iss)

Winter Aconite

RANUNCULACEAE; buttercup family

Height/habit: 3–6 in. (7.5–15 cm.).
Leaves: Solitary, lobed, peltate leaf, to 2 in. (5 cm.) across; stands rufflike atop each stem.
Flowers: Single, cupped, 1–2 in. (2.5–5 cm.) across; bright yellow.
Season: During winter thaws or earliest spring; disappears by late spring.

When to plant: Set bulbs 3–4 in. (7.5–10 cm.) deep, 3 in. (7.5 cm.) apart as soon as they are available in fall. Cold-hardy zone 6 but not recommended zone 9 and warmer.
Light: Half sun to half shade.
Soil: Well drained; moist through spring, on the dry side in summer.
Fertilizer: 5-10-5.
Storage: Store in damp peat moss at 40–50°F (4–10°C), as briefly as possible, until planting time.
Propagation: By normal increase, usually self-sown seedlings.
Uses: Wild or rock gardens.

EREMURUS
(air-ee-MEW-russ)

Desert Candle; Foxtail Lily

LILIACEAE; lily family

Height/habit: Raceme rises 4–6 ft. (1.2–1.8 m.).

Leaves: Strap-shaped and narrow, to 15–20 in. (38–50 cm.) long, in tufts or rosettes; basal foliage to 2 ft. (61 cm.) high/wide.

Flowers: Showy, blooming profusely in small bell shapes on long spikes; orange, pink, white, or yellow.

Season: Late spring through early summer.

When to plant: Set the fleshy roots in fall, with the growth eye 4–6 in. (10–15 cm.) deep 1.5–2 ft. (45–61 cm.) apart. Winter-hardy zone 7 and warmer but not suited to the mild, humid Gulf Coast.

Light: Sun half day or more.

Soil: Well drained; moist in spring, on the dry side throughout summer.

Fertilizer: 5-10-5.

Storage: Store roots in dry peat moss at 50–60°F (10–15°C), as briefly as possible, from receipt until planting time.

Propagation: Sow seeds as soon as they ripen in summer or divide roots in fall.

Uses: Back of border or as accent in a rock garden; cut flowers.

ERYTHRONIUM
(air-ee-THROW-nee-um)

Dogtooth Violet; Trout Lily

LILIACEAE; lily family

Height/habit: Slender flower stalks rise to 1 ft. (30 cm.) from a pair of basal leaves.
Leaves: Tongue-shaped, 6–12 in. (15–30 cm.) long; often mottled purple, brown, or white.
Flowers: Lilylike, 1–2 in. (2.5–5 cm.) across; white, pink, yellow, rose, purple, cream, sometimes with contrasting color in the throat.

Season: Spring.
When to plant: Set the small corms 3 in. (7.5 cm.) deep, 6 in. (15 cm.) apart, in fall and leave undisturbed as long as possible. Since these American natives are on the preservation lists of numerous states, purchase corms certified to have originated in a nursery. Ground-hardy zone 5 and warmer but not suited to warm, humid Gulf Coast gardens.
Light: Half sun to half shade; ideal under deciduous trees.
Soil: Humusy, deep, well drained, moist.

Fertilizer: 5-10-5 or 14-14-14 to help them become established.
Storage: Store corms in dry peat moss at 50–60°F (10–15°C), as briefly as possible, from receipt until planting time.
Propagation: Remove bulb offsets or sow seeds in fall.
Uses: Wild or rock gardens, beds, borders.

EUCHARIS
(YEW-kah-riss)

Amazon Lily; Eucharist Lily

AMARYLLIDACEAE; amaryllis family

Height/habit: Clumps of dark green leaves resembling those of spathiphyllum (peace lily, or closet plant), 1–2 ft. (30–61 cm.) high/wide.

Leaves: Rise directly from the bulb, first a slender stalk, then reaching 6 in. (15 cm.) wide by twice as long. After a season the oldest die down naturally.

Flowers: To 4 in. (10 cm.) across, several atop each smooth stalk, 1.5–2 ft. (20–61 cm.) high; white with touches of green in the throat; lemon-scented flowers resemble daffodils.

Season: Spring in Southern gardens; at various times during the year for potted specimens, which can be alternatively pushed to promote leaf production, then dried out for a few weeks, followed by regular watering and fertilizer, which promotes a round of bloom.

When to plant: Set dormant bulbs with the neck slightly exposed, 6–12 in. (15–30 cm.) apart, when available; potted specimens with leaves are a better investment. Ground-hardy zone 10 and warmer, elsewhere best grown in a pot.

Light: Half sun to half shade.

Soil: Humusy, well drained; moist, except on the dry side after a season of leaf production.

Fertilizer: 5-10-5 or 14-14-14.

Storage: Store bulbs in dry peat moss at 50–60°F (10–15°C), as briefly as possible, from receipt until planting time.

Propagation: Divide established clumps at repotting time in early spring.

Uses: Beds, borders, pots, cut flowers.

EUCOMIS
(yew-KOH-miss)

Pineapple Lily

LILIACEAE; lily family

Height/habit: Basal rosettes
1–2 ft. (30–61 cm.) high/wide
with flower stalks rising
slightly higher.

Leaves: Strap-shaped, wavy-
edged, 1–2 ft. (30–61 cm.) long,
2–3 in. (5–7.5 cm.) wide.

Flowers: Dense raceme or
spike along the upper third of
the scape, 1–1.5 ft. (30–45 cm.)
high, crowned by a leafy
rosette, reminiscent of a
pineapple; creamy to greenish
with thin purple edging.

Season: Mid- to late summer.

When to plant: Set the bulbs
1 in. (2.5 cm.) deep, 8–12 in.
(20–30 cm.) apart in spring,
after the weather is warm and
settled. Ground-hardy zone 8
and warmer. Elsewhere treat
as gladiolus.

Light: Sun half day or more.

Soil: Humusy, moist, well
drained.

Fertilizer: 5-10-5 or 14-14-14.

Storage: Store bulbs in dry
peat moss at 50–60°F (10–15°C)
during freezing weather.

Propagation: Remove offsets
in spring or sow seeds.

Uses: Beds, borders, pots,
cut flowers.

EUCROSIA
(yew-KROH-zee-ah)

Eucrosia

AMARYLLIDACEAE; amaryllis
family

Height/habit: Tidy clumps,
1–1.5 ft. (30–45 cm.) high/wide.
Leaves: Narrow stalks arise
from the bulb, then flare to
2–3 in. (5–7.5 cm.) wide by
6–8 in. (15–20 cm.) long; also
rounded.
Flowers: Distinguished by long
yellow stamens extending
noticeably beyond the corolla
tube, up to a dozen atop each
scape, 1–2 in (2.5–5 cm.) across;
reddish orange.
Season: Fall or early winter;
also blooms at various times
under the regimen set out for
Eucharis, a closely related
plant.
When to plant: Set bulbs or
transplants when available;
position so that the neck of
the bulb is just above the soil,
6–12 in. (15–30 cm.) apart.
Ground-hardy zone 10 and
warmer; elsewhere grow
in pots.
Light: Half sun to half shade.
Soil: Humusy, well drained;
moist while in bloom; on the
dry side during the summer
resting period.
Fertilizer: 5-10-5 or 14-14-14.
Storage: Store bulbs in dry
peat moss at 60°F (15°C),
as briefly as possible, until
planting time.
Propagation: Divide established clumps or sow seeds
in fall or spring.
Uses: Beds, borders, pots,
cut flowers.

FREESIA
(FREE-zee-ah)
Freesia
IRIDACEAE; iris family

Height/habit: Small clumps, 1–1.5 ft. (30–45 cm.) high/wide.
Leaves: Sword-shaped and grassy, 6–18 in. (15–45 cm.) long, to 1 in. (2.5 cm.) wide.
Flowers: Borne on distinctive 1-sided spikes, tubular, each to 2 in. (5 cm.) long; single or double; white, yellow, pink, red, lavender, purple, orange, or blue; whites and yellows most dependably fragrant.
Season: Winter in mild climate, cool window, or greenhouse; summer in cold climates having relatively cool summers.
When to plant: Set corms 2 in. (5 cm.) deep, 2 in. (5 cm.) apart in early fall for indoor pots or in the ground (mild climates); in cold regions set corms outdoors in spring, as with gladiolus. Ground-hardy zone 9 and warmer. Common white freesia naturalizes best along the Gulf Coast.
Light: Sun half day or more.
Soil: Well drained; moist while in active growth, on the dry side during other seasons.
Fertilizer: 5-10-5 or 14-14-14.
Storage: Store corms in dry peat moss at 50–60°F (10–15°C) from receipt until planting time.
Propagation: Remove offsets or sow seeds in fall or spring.
Uses: Beds, borders, pots, cut flowers.

FRITILLARIA
(frit-ill-LAY-ree-ah)

Crown Imperial; Checkered Lily

LILIACEAE; lily family

Height/habit: Crown imperial (*F. imperialis*) types produce a strong, upright stalk 3–4 ft. (1–1.2 m.), crowned by flowers, with a tuft of leaves on top; checkered lily (*F. meleagris*) types much smaller, graceful, 1–1.5 ft. (30–45 cm.).

Leaves: Lance-shaped in crown imperial, to 6 in. (15 cm.) long; narrow and linear in checkered lily, 3–6 in. (7.5–15 cm.) long.

Flowers: Nodding bells, to 2 in. (5 cm.) across, clustered at the top of the stalk in crown imperial; solitary or up to 3 atop a wiry stem in checkered lily; scarlet to orange or yellow in crown imperial (with skunklike odor that is compensated for by beauty of blooms); veined or checkered reddish purple to white in checkered lily.

Season: Spring.

When to plant: Set bulbs in fall: larger ones (crown imperial) 4–6 in. (10–15 cm.) deep, 1 ft. (30 cm.) apart; smaller ones (checkered lily) 3–4 in. (7.5–10 cm.) deep, 6 in. (15 cm.) apart. Ground-hardy zones 5–9; rarely successful after the first season.

Light: Sun half day or more.

Soil: Well drained; moist while in active growth, on the dry side during other seasons.

Fertilizer: 5-10-5 or 14-14-14.

Storage: Store bulbs in dry peat moss at 40–50°F (4–10°C) from receipt until planting time.

Propagation: Remove offsets in fall.

Uses: Beds, borders, cut flowers.

GALANTHUS
(gay-LANTH-us)

Snowdrop

AMARYLLIDACEAE; amaryllis family

Height/habit: Short, erect, 6–8 in. (15–20 cm.).
Leaves: 2–3 from each bulb, 4–6 in. (10–15 cm.) long.
Flowers: Dangling bells, 1–2 in. (2.5–5 cm.) long; white, often with distinctive green markings between the petals.
Season: Winter thaws or earliest spring.
When to plant: Set bulbs 2–4 in. (5–10 cm.) deep, 2–4 in. (5–10 cm.) apart in early fall. Ground-hardy zones 2–3 and farther south; short-lived zones 8–9 and warmer.
Light: Full sun to part shade.
Soil: Well drained, moist.
Fertilizer: 5-10-5.
Storage: Store bulbs in dry peat moss at 40–50°F (4–10°C), as briefly as possible, from receipt until planting time.
Propagation: Divide bulb clumps in early fall.
Uses: Beds, borders, wild and rock gardens, cut flowers.

GALTONIA
(gal-TOH-nee-ah)

Summer Hyacinth

LILIACEAE; lily family

Height/habit: Resembling gladiolus, erect, 3–4 ft. (1–1.2 m.).
Leaves: Sword-shaped, to 1 ft. (30 cm.) long.
Flowers: Bells, 1 in. (2.5 cm.) long, appear along upper half of a straight stalk; white; fragrant.
Season: Late summer through early fall in cold climates, spring through early summer along the Gulf Coast.
When to plant: Set bulbs 6 in. (15 cm.) deep, 6–12 in. (15–30 cm.) apart in spring. Ground-hardy zone 5 with deep winter mulch, elsewhere to zones 9–10.
Light: Full sun to part shade.
Soil: Well drained, moist.
Fertilizer: 5-10-5.
Storage: Store bulbs in dry peat moss at 50–60°F (10–15°C), as briefly as possible, from receipt until planting time.
Propagation: Remove offsets or seeds in spring.
Uses: Beds, borders, cut flowers.

GLADIOLUS
(glad-ee-OH-luss)

Corn Flag; Sword Lily

IRIDACEAE; iris family

Height/habit: Clumps; spikes reach 2–6 ft. (61–180 cm.).
Leaves: Sword-shaped, erect, grassy; 1–2 ft. (30–61 cm.) long.
Flowers: Open from bottom up on a 1-sided spike; quite stiffly presented in large-flowered hybrids; much smaller (about 1.5 in. [3.7 cm.] long) and more graceful in the species and hardy types; *G. tristis* fragrant; almost all colors.
Season: Spring and fall in mild-winter, hot-summer gardens; summer elsewhere.

When to plant: Spring through early summer in cold climates; at almost any time the corms are available in mild-winter areas. Set corms 3–6 in. (7.5–15 cm.) deep, the same distance apart.
Light: Sun half day or more.
Soil: Well drained, moist.
Fertilizer: 5-10-5.
Storage: Store corms in dry peat moss at 50–60°F (10–15°C) from fall through winter until planting time.
Propagation: Remove cormlets or sow seeds in spring.
Uses: Beds, borders, pots, cut flowers.

GLOBBA
(GLOB-bah)
Dancing Lady Ginger
ZINGIBERACEAE; ginger family

Height/habit: Upright clumps 1.5–2 ft. (20–61 cm.) high/wide.
Leaves: Lance-shaped, to 8 in. (20 cm.) long x 2 in. (5 cm.) wide; bright green.
Flowers: Appear in pendant racemes; yellow with reflexed purple bracts.
Season: Summer through early fall.
When to plant: Set tubers 2 in. (5 cm.) deep, 2 in. (5 cm.) apart in spring, or when the soil is warm. Ground-hardy zone 9 and warmer. Elsewhere, grow in pots and bring inside during winter.
Light: Half sun to half shade.
Soil: Humusy, well drained; moist while in active growth, quite dry when dormant.
Fertilizer: 5-10-5.
Storage: Store roots from fall through winter in dry peat moss at 60°F (15°C); alternatively, dry in the pots where they are established.
Propagation: Divide in spring.
Uses: Beds, borders, pots.

GLORIOSA
(gloh-ree-OH-sah)
Climbing Lily
LILIACEAE; lily family

Height/habit: Tendril-climbing to 6 ft. (1.8 m.).
Leaves: Lance-shaped, extending into a long tip that acts as a climbing tendril.
Flowers: Recurved, often wavy edged, to 3 in. (7.5 cm.) across; red, yellow, apricot, or bicolored.
Season: Spring, summer, or fall, depending on the species and growing conditions.
When to plant: Set tubers 2 in. (5 cm.) deep, 1 ft. (30 cm.) apart (or in sufficiently large pots to accommodate their long cigar shape) in spring or summer. Ground-hardy zone 9 and warmer.
Light: Sun half day or more.
Soil: Humusy, well drained; moist during the active growing season.
Fertilizer: 5-10-5.
Storage: Store tubers in dry peat moss at 60°F (15°C) from fall through winter until planting time.
Propagation: Remove offsets and tuber divisions or sow seeds in spring.
Uses: For ornamenting fences, trellises, lattice structures; cut flowers.

GLOXINIA
(glox-IN-ee-ah)

True Gloxinia

GESNERIACEAE; gesneriad family

Height/habit: Bushy or upright, 1–2 ft. (30–61 cm.).

Leaves: Ovate, hairy, to 3–4 in. (7.5–10 cm.) long.

Flowers: Funnel- to bell-shaped, 1–2 in. (2.5–5 cm.) long; rose pink with red spots, lavender with purple throat.

Season: Summer through early fall.

When to plant: Set scaly rhizomes 1–2 in. (2.5–5 cm.) deep, 3–4 in. (7.5–10 cm.) apart in spring, or when the soil is warm. Ground-hardy zone 10 and warmer; elsewhere, grow potted.

Light: Half sun to half shade.

Soil: Humusy, well drained; moist while active, nearly dry while resting.

Fertilizer: 5-10-5.

Storage: Store scaly rhizomes in dry peat moss at 50–60°F (10–15°C) from fall through winter until planting time.

Propagation: By natural increase of the rhizomes; alternatively, sow individual scales as "seeds" in warm nursery conditions.

Uses: Beds, borders, mostly in pots.

HABRANTHUS
(hay-BRANTH-us)

Rain Lily

AMARYLLIDACEAE; amaryllis family

Height/habit: Grassy clumps, 8–12 in. (20–30 cm.) high/wide.

Leaves: Narrow blades, 8–12 in. (20–30 cm.) long.

Flowers: Trumpet-shaped, 2–3 in. (5–7.5 cm.) across; pale to dark pink and rose, yellow, copper, or white.

Season: Summer or autumn, often following rain that ends a period of dry weather.

When to plant: Set bulbs 1–2 in. (2.5–5 cm.) deep, 3–6 in. (7.5–15 cm.) apart in spring; set transplants as available. Ground-hardy zone 9 and warmer. Elsewhere, grow in pots or dig before frost.

Light: Sun to half shade.

Soil: Well drained, moist to on the dry side.

Fertilizer: 5-10-5.

Storage: Store in dry peat moss at 50–60°F (10–15°C) only from receipt until planting time.

Propagation: Remove offsets in spring or summer, or sow seeds as soon as they are ripe.

Uses: Beds, borders, wild and rock gardens, pots.

HAEMANTHUS
(hay-MANTH-us)
White Paintbrush
AMARYLLIDACEAE; amaryllis
family

Height/habit: Upright, to 1 ft.
(30 cm.).
Leaves: Broad straps, 8–10 in.
(20–25 cm.) long x 3–4 in.
(7.5–10 cm.) wide in most
haemanthus; finely haired in
white paintbrush (*N. albiflos*).
Flowers: Appear in a dense
umbel, 2–3 in. (5–7.5 cm.)
wide, with protruding yellow
stamens; white in white paintbrush, scarlet red in others
(see also *Scadoxus*).
Season: Fall through winter,
or following 2–3 months of
dryness.

When to plant: Set bulbs with
the tips exposed, 1 ft. (30 cm.)
apart; set transplants when
available. Disturb established
haemanthus as little as possible. Winter-hardy zone 9 and
warmer.
Light: Sun half day or more.
Soil: Humusy, well drained;
moist, except on the dry side
from fall through winter.
Fertilizer: 5-10-5.
Storage: Store in dry peat
moss at 50–60°F (10–15°C), as
briefly as possible, until planting time. Do not deprive evergreen species of light.
Propagation: Remove offsets
when active growth begins.
Uses: Beds, borders, pots.

HEDYCHIUM
(heh-DICK-ee-um)
Butterfly Ginger
ZINGIBERACEAE; ginger family

Height/habit: Upright, 3–10 ft.
(1–10 m.), forming colonies of
about the same width.
Leaves: Broadly lance-shaped,
to 10–24 in. (25–61 cm.) long x
4–10 in. (10–25 cm.) wide.
Flowers: 2–3 in. (5–7.5 cm.)
across in spikes at the top of
each leafy, bamboolike stalk;
fragrant; white, orange, coral
red, or pale yellow.
Season: Summer through fall.
When to plant: Set rhizomes
at beginning of warm season,
1–3 in. (2.5–7.5 cm.) deep,
1–2 ft. (30–61 cm.) apart; set
transplants when available.
Ground-hardy zone 9 and
warmer.

Light: Half sun to half shade.
Soil: Humusy, well drained,
moist.
Fertilizer: 5-10-5.
Storage: Store rhizomes in dry
peat moss at 50–60°F (10–15°C),
as briefly as possible, from
receipt until planting time.
Propagation: Divide bulbs in
spring.
Uses: Beds, borders, pots;
exceptional for partly shaded
summer gardens in hot
climates.

HELICONIA
(hell-ick-OH-nee-ah)

Lobster Claws

HELICONIACEAE; heliconia family

Height/habit: Erect, 10–15 ft. (3–4.5 m.), forming colonies. Dwarfs only 1.5 ft. (45 cm.).

Leaves: Paddle-shaped on long stalks, each 2–4 ft. (61–122 cm.) long; reminiscent of bird of paradise (*Strelitzia*) and banana (*Musa*).

Flowers: Bloom from colorful, boat-shaped bracts, 5–10 in. (12.5–25 cm.) long; variously erect or pendulous; yellow, orange, or red.

Season: Summer through fall, or during any warm period.

When to plant: Set transplants when available. Hardy zone 10 and warmer.

Light: Half sun to half shade.

Soil: Humusy, well drained, moist.

Fertilizer: 5-10-5.

Storage: Not feasible; evergreen leaves need light, warmth (60°F [10–15°C]), and moisture.

Propagation: Divide at beginning of summer.

Uses: Beds, borders, pots, cut flowers.

HIPPEASTRUM
(hip-pee-AST-rum)

Florists' Amaryllis; Dutch Amaryllis

AMARYLLIDACEAE; amaryllis family

Height/habit: Upright, 1–4 ft. (30–122 cm.), forming colonies.

Leaves: Strap-shaped, 1–4 ft. (30–122 cm.) long, 1–4 in. (2.5–10 cm.) wide; variously evergreen or deciduous.

Flowers: Trumpets, single or double, 2–10 in. (5–25 cm.) across; some fragrant; most colors except true blue.

Season: Fall through winter if newly purchased, otherwise winter through spring.

When to plant: Set bulbs with the neck and some shoulder above ground, 1–2 ft. (30–61 cm.) apart, in fall through winter or as available. Ground-hardy zone 8 and warmer.

Light: Sun half day or more.

Soil: Humusy, well drained; moist, except one season of dryness, usually fall through winter.

Fertilizer: 5-10-5, 14-14-14.

Storage: Store bulbs in dry peat moss at 50–60°F (10–15°C) from receipt until planting time. Do not deprive evergreen types of light or dry off to the point of yellowing all the leaves.

Propagation: Remove offsets at repotting time or sow seeds as soon as ripe.

Uses: Beds, borders, pots, cut flowers.

HYACINTHOIDES
(high-ah-sin-THOY-deez)

English Bluebell; Spanish Bluebell

LILIACEAE; lily family

Height/habit: Upright 1–1.5 ft. (30–45 cm.); at first in tidy clumps, later colonizing.
Leaves: Strap-shaped to 1 ft. (30 cm.) long, rising directly from the base.
Flowers: Erect racemes, each to 2 in. (5 cm.) across, bell-like; fragrant; blue, white, or pink. Sometimes also known as *Scilla* and *Endymion*.
Season: Late spring.
When to plant: Set bulbs 2–4 in. (5–10 cm.) deep, 4–6 in. (10–15 cm.) apart in fall. Ground-hardy zone 5 and warmer.
Light: Half sun to half shade.
Soil: Well drained; moist fall through spring, dryness acceptable in summer.
Fertilizer: 5-10-5.
Storage: Store bulbs in dry peat moss at 40–50°F (4–10°C) from receipt until planting time.
Propagation: Remove offsets at fall planting time.
Uses: Beds, borders, wild gardens, cut flowers. Often interplanted with hostas and hardy ferns.

HYACINTHUS
(high-ah-SINTH-us)

Hyacinth

LILIACEAE; lily family

Height/habit: Upright, 8–18 in. (20–45 cm.).

Leaves: Strap-shaped, rising directly from the base, 8–14 in. (20–35 cm.) long x 1–2 in. (2.5–5 cm.) wide.

Flowers: Appear in dense racemes at the top of a succulent stalk; single or double, each to 1 in. (2.5 cm.) across; fragrant; most colors, including outstanding blues.

Season: Spring. Much favored for forcing into winter bloom indoors.

When to plant: Set bulbs 4–6 in. (10–15 cm.) deep, 6–8 in. (15–20 cm.) apart in fall. Cold-hardy zone 6 and warmer but not reliable for repeat performance zone 8 or warmer.

Light: Sun half day or more.

Soil: Well drained, moist.

Fertilizer: 5-10-5.

Storage: Store bulbs in dry peat moss at 40–50°F (4–10°C) from receipt until planting time.

Propagation: Remove offsets.

Uses: Beds, borders, pots, cut flowers, forcing.

HYMENOCALLIS
(high-men-OCK-al-liss)
Spider Lily
AMARYLLIDACEAE; amaryllis family

Height/habit: Upright, 1–3 ft. (30–90 cm.).
Leaves: Strap-shaped, 1–2 ft. (30–61 cm.) long, 1–2 in. (2.5–5 cm.) wide.
Flowers: Long, spidery petals grow from a daffodil-like cup, each to 5–6 in. (12.5–15 cm.) across; fragrant; white.
Season: Summer.
When to plant: Set bulbs 4–6 in. (10–15 cm.) deep, 6–8 in. (15–20 cm.) apart in spring; set transplants when available. Ground-hardy zone 9 and warmer. Elsewhere, dig and bring inside before hard frost in autumn.
Light: Sun half day or more.
Soil: Humusy, well drained; moist to wet while in active growth.
Fertilizer: 5-10-5.
Storage: Store bulbs in dry peat moss at 50–60°F (10–15°C) from receipt until planting time.
Propagation: Divide bulbs in spring.
Uses: Beds, borders, pots, cut flowers.

IPHEION
(IF-fee-on)
Spring Starflower
AMARYLLIDACEAE; amaryllis family

Height/habit: Grassy clumps, 6–8 in. (15–20 cm.), rapidly colonizing.
Leaves: Narrow, strap-shaped, 6–8 in. (15–20 cm.) long, smelling of onion.
Flowers: Star-shaped, 1–2 in. (2.5–5 cm.) across, standing slightly above the leaves; white tinged blue or lavender.
Season: Spring.
When to plant: Set bulbs 1–2 in. (2.5–5 cm.) deep, 2–4 in. (5–10 cm.) apart in fall. Ground-hardy zone 6 and warmer. Colonizes freely through zone 9.
Light: Sun to half shade.
Soil: Well drained; moist fall through spring, dryness acceptable in summer.
Fertilizer: 5-10-5.
Storage: Store bulbs in dry peat moss at 40–50°F (4–10°C) from receipt until planting time.
Propagation: Remove offsets at fall planting time or sow seeds.
Uses: Beds, borders, rock and wild gardens.

IPOMOEA
(ipp-oh-MEE-ah)

Sweet Potato Vine

CONVOLVULACEAE; morning-glory family

Height/habit: Trailing, stem-rooting vine.
Leaves: Variously oval, triangular, or digitately lobed, to 3 in. (7.5 cm.) long, blackish green in the cultivar 'Blackie.'
Flowers: Inconspicuous.
Season: Summer until frost.
When to plant: At beginning of warm weather, set root cuttings or tubers or tuber pieces with eyes 1–2 in. (2.5–5 cm.) deep, 6–8 in. (15–20 cm.) apart. Ground-hardy zone 9 and warmer.
Light: Sun to half shade.
Soil: Humusy, well drained, moist.
Fertilizer: 5-10-5.
Storage: Store tubers in dry peat moss at 50–60°F (10–15°C) from receipt until planting time.
Propagation: Divide tubers at planting time or propagate from cuttings.
Uses: Beds, borders, ground cover, hanging baskets.

IRIS
(EYE-riss)

Dutch, German, Japanese, and Louisiana Irises

IRIDACEAE; iris family

Height/habit: Grassy, upright, 8–48 in. (20–122 cm.).
Leaves: Narrow spears, about 9–12 in. (22.5–30 cm.) long.
Flowers: Similar to a fleur-de-lis, consisting of 3 standards and 3 falls, 1–8 in. (2.5–20 cm.) across; often fragrant; all colors, many bicolors and blends (especially with Japanese iris [*I. kaempferi*]).
Season: Spring.
When to plant: Set corms, rhizomes, or divisions in late summer or fall; set transplants as available. Set corms 2–4 in. (5–10 cm.) deep, 4–6 in. (10–15 cm.) apart. Gardeners often set rhizomes and divisions in groups of 3, in order to produce a big show beginning the second season. German iris (*I. germanica*) handsome in clumps. Cold-hardy zone 6 and warmer; Louisiana iris (*I. fulva* and others) favored in zone 8 and warmer, especially along the Gulf Coast.
Light: Sun to half shade.
Soil: Humusy, well drained; moist, except on the dry side following the blooming season.
Fertilizer: 5-10-5.
Storage: Store corms in dry peat moss at 40–50°F (4–10°C) from receipt until planting time.
Propagation: Divide or sow seeds.
Uses: Beds, borders, ground cover, containers, cut flowers. Dutch iris (*I. xiphium*) forced for winter bloom.

Peacock Ginger

ZINGIBERACEAE; ginger family

Height/habit: Leafy ground cover, to 1.5 ft. (45 cm.).

Leaves: Broadly oval to rounded, 8–10 in. (20–25 cm.) long/wide; highly variegated in *K. roscoeana*, resembling taffeta fabric.

Flowers: Bloom for 1 day, appearing from the base of the leaves or on upright stalks, each 1–3 in. (2.5–7.5 cm.) across; lavender blue or yellow.

Season: Summer.

When to plant: Set tubers 1 in. (2.5 cm.) deep, 8–12 in. (20–30 cm.) apart at the beginning of warm weather. Set transplants when available. Ground-hardy zone 9 and warmer.

Light: Half to full shade.

Soil: Humusy, well drained; moist, except on the dry side in winter.

Fertilizer: 5-10-5.

Storage: Store tuberous roots in dry peat moss at 50–60°F (10–15°C) from fall through winter until planting time. Potted kaempferias can be left in their containers, kept dry and moderately warm through their winter dormancy.

Propagation: Divide in spring.

Uses: Beds, borders, ground cover, pots.

KNIPHOFIA
(nipp-HOH-fee-ah)

Tritoma;
Torch Lily;
Red-hot Poker

LILIACEAE; lily family

Height/habit: Grassy clumps; flowers rise high above, to 4 ft. (1.2 m.).

Leaves: Long, narrow spears, 1–1.5 ft. (30–45 cm.) long.

Flowers: Tubular with noticeable stamens, densely packed at the top of rigid, showy stalks, 10 in. (25 cm.) long; yellow, cream, chartreuse, orange, or red.

Season: Summer.

When to plant: Set rhizomatous roots or transplants in spring, at the beginning of the growing season, with the eyes barely covered 1.5 ft. (45 cm.) apart. Ground-hardy zone 6; heat-tolerant through zones 9–10.

Light: Sun half day or more.

Soil: Well drained, moist to on the dry side.

Fertilizer: 5-10-5.

Storage: Store roots in dry peat moss at 40–50°F (4–10°C) from receipt until planting time.

Propagation: Divide in spring or sow seeds.

Uses: Beds, borders, pots, cut flowers.

KOHLERIA
(koh-LEAR-ee-ah)

Isoloma; Tree Gloxinia

GESNERIACEAE; gesneriad family

Height/habit: Bushy, self-branching, 1–2.5 ft. (30–76 cm.) high/wide.

Leaves: Ovate, 1–2 in. (2.5–5 cm.) long, velvety-hairy to the touch, growing along upright stems.

Flowers: Numerous nodding bells, 1–2 in. (2.5–5 cm.) across; orange, red, yellow, or pink.

Season: Summer or at any season if potted and provided with sufficient warmth, humidity, and light; tip cuttings often bloom in fluorescent-light gardens when quite tiny.

When to plant: Set scaly rhizomes 1–2 in. (2.5–5 cm.) deep, 2–4 in. (5–10 cm.) apart at the beginning of a warm season. Ground-hardy zone 10 and warmer.

Light: Half sun to half shade.

Soil: Humusy, well drained; moist, except on the dry side while resting.

Fertilizer: 5-10-5.

Storage: Store scaly rhizomes in dry peat moss at 50–60°F (10–15°C) from fall through winter until planting time.

Propagation: Divide rhizomes at planting time or sow seeds.

Uses: Beds, borders, pots.

LACHENALIA
(lack-en-NAY-lee-ah)

Cape Cowslip

LILIACEAE; lily family

Height/habit: Fleshy leaves appear in a basal rosette, resembling hyacinth, to 1 ft. (30 cm.).

Leaves: Strap-shaped, green or with silvery variegation, 6–12 in. (15–30 cm.) long.

Flowers: Nodding, tubular, to 1 in. (2.5 cm.), in racemes above the leaves; yellow, scarlet, often green-tipped.

Season: Winter through spring.

When to plant: Set bulbs 2 in. (5 cm.) deep, 4–6 in. (10–15 cm.) apart in fall. Ground-hardy zone 9 and warmer.

Light: Sun half day or more.

Soil: Well drained; moist fall through spring, dry during summer rest.

Fertilizer: 5-10-5.

Storage: Store bulbs in dry peat moss at 50–60°F (10–15°C) in summer through planting time.

Propagation: Remove offsets at planting time or sow seeds.

Uses: Beds, borders, pots, cut flowers.

LEDEBOURIA
(led-eh-BOO-ree-ah)

Silver Squill

LILIACEAE; lily family

Height/habit: Clump-forming bulbous plant, 6–8 in. (15–20 cm.) high/wide.

Leaves: Succulent straps, 2–4 in. (5–10 cm.) long x 1 in. (2.5 cm.) wide; silver spotted, olive green above, wine red below.

Flowers: Quite small in slender racemes 6–8 in. (15–20 cm.) long; green and blue. Sometimes known as *Scilla violacea*.

Season: Winter for flowers; leaves attractive at most times.

When to plant: Set bulbs 1 in. (2.5 cm.) deep, 2–4 in. (5–10 cm.) apart in fall; set transplants when available. Ground-hardy zone 10 and warmer; elsewhere this makes an outstanding houseplant.

Light: Sun half day or more.

Soil: Well drained, moist to on the dry side.

Fertilizer: 5-10-5.

Storage: Store in dry peat moss at 50–60°F (10–15°C), as briefly as possible, from receipt until planting time.

Propagation: Remove offsets in spring or summer.

Uses: Beds, borders, rock gardens, pots, houseplant.

LEUCOJUM
(LEW-koh-jum)

Snowflake

AMARYLLIDACEAE; amaryllis family

Height/habit: Grassy clumps to 1 ft. (30 cm.) high/wide.

Leaves: Narrow straps, 8–16 in. (20–40 cm.) long.

Flowers: Nodding bells, to 1 in. (2.5 cm.) across; white, green-tipped.

Season: Early spring for *L. vernalis*; late spring for *L. aestivum*; fall for *L. autumnale*.

When to plant: Set bulbs 2–4 in. (5–10 cm.) deep, 4–6 in. (10–15 cm.) apart in fall; set transplants when available. Ground-hardy zones 4–5 and warmer. *L. aestivum* colonizes in gardens along the Gulf Coast zone 9 and warmer; *L. autumnale* does better zone 8 and colder.

Light: Sun to half shade.

Soil: Well drained; moist; after flowering and foliage development, dryness is acceptable.

Fertilizer: 5-10-5.

Storage: Store bulbs in dry peat moss at 40–60°F (4–15°C), as briefly as possible, from receipt until planting time.

Propagation: Remove offsets at planting time. Leucojums are best left undisturbed indefinitely.

Uses: Beds, borders, wild gardens, cut flowers.

LILIUM
(LIL-e-um)
Lily
LILIACEAE; lily family

Height/habit: Upright stalks clothed by many leaves and crowned by numerous flowers, 1–8 ft. (30–240 cm.).

Leaves: Narrow, 3–5 in. (7.5–12.5 cm.) long.

Flowers: Trumpets or reflexed petals, 2–8 in. (5–20 cm.) wide; fragrant; white, pink, rose, red, orange, yellow, lavender, often with contrasting spots or margins.

Season: Spring until early fall, depending on the lineage.

When to plant: Set bulbs 6–8 in. (15–20 cm.) deep, 8–12 in. (20–30 cm.) apart in fall or early spring. Ground-hardy zone 6 and warmer. Bermuda Easter lily (*L. longifolium*) and Formosa lily (*L. formosanum*) thrive along Gulf Coast and other mild regions (zone 9 and warmer).

Light: Sun to half shade.

Soil: Humusy, well drained, moist.

Fertilizer: 5-10-5.

Storage: Store bulbs in dry peat moss at 40–50°F (4–10°C), as briefly as possible, from receipt until planting time.

Propagation: Remove offsets at planting time or sow seeds.

Uses: Beds, borders, pots, cut flowers.

LYCORIS
(leye-KOH-riss)

Naked Lady; Hurricane Lily

AMARYLLIDACEAE; amaryllis family

Height/habit: Foliage, 1–1.5 ft. (30–45 cm.), followed by flower stalks, 15–30 in. (38–76 cm.).
Leaves: Narrow straps, to 1 ft. (30 cm.) long; appear in spring and die down in summer, followed by flowers.
Flowers: Spidery-looking, each to 2 in. (5 cm.) across; bloom in umbels atop a rigid scape; red, pink, yellow, or white.
Season: Late summer early fall.
When to plant: Set the bulbs 2–4 in. (5–10 cm.) deep, 6 in. (15 cm.) apart in late summer or fall; set transplants when available in spring. *L. squamigera* is ground-hardy zone 5 and warmer, the others zone 8 and warmer. *L. radiata* has naturalized in gardens throughout the Southeastern United States.
Light: Sun to half shade.
Soil: Well drained; moist, except summer dryness acceptable.
Fertilizer: 5-10-5.
Storage: Store bulbs in dry peat moss at 50–60°F (10–15°C) from receipt until planting time.
Propagation: Remove offsets at planting time in the fall.
Uses: Beds, borders, pots, cut flowers.

MUSCARI
(moos-KAH-ree)
Grape Hyacinth
LILIACEAE; lily family

Height/habit: Grassy leaves stay close to the ground with flowers rising just above on slender, erect spikes, 6–10 in. (15–25 cm.).

Leaves: Long, narrow, grassy, to 8–10 in. (20–25 cm.), appearing in fall and persisting through the spring blooming season.

Flowers: Urn-shaped and tiny, .75 in. (2 cm.) across; bloom in fragrant spires; blue, purple, or white.

Season: Early to midspring. Excellent for forcing earlier in pots indoors.

When to plant: Set bulbs 2–4 in. (5–10 cm.) deep, 4–6 in. (10–15 cm.) apart in early fall. Ground-hardy zone 5 and warmer; might not return in zone 9 and warmer.

Light: Sun to half shade.

Soil: Well drained, moist, except summer dryness acceptable.

Fertilizer: 5-10-5.

Storage: Store bulbs in dry peat moss at 40–50°F (4–10°C) from receipt until planting time.

Propagation: Remove offsets at planting time or sow seeds.

Uses: Beds, borders, pots, cut flowers, forcing.

NARCISSUS
(nar-SISS-us)

Daffodil; Telephone Flower

AMARYLLIDACEAE; amaryllis family

Height/habit: Grassy clumps, 6–18 in. (15–45 cm.) high/wide.
Leaves: Narrow, grasslike, 6–18 in. (15–45 cm.) long.
Flowers: Shallow to deep cups surrounded by petals, single or double; tubes 1–2 in. (2.5–5 cm.) long; fragrant; white, yellow, orange, or pink.
Season: Primarily spring in cold climates; fall through winter and early spring zone 9 and warmer. Can be forced indoors ahead of outdoor blooming season.
When to plant: Set bulbs 4–6 in. (10–15 cm.) deep, 3–6 in. (7.5–15 cm.) apart in early fall.
Light: Sun to half shade.
Soil: Well drained; moist, except summer dryness acceptable.
Fertilizer: 5-10-5.
Storage: Store bulbs in dry peat moss at 40–50°F (4–10°C) only from receipt until planting time.
Propagation: Remove offsets at planting time.
Uses: Beds, borders, wild and rock gardens, forcing, cut flowers.

NEOMARICA
(nee-oh-mah-REEK-ah)
Walking Iris; Twelve Apostles
IRIDACEAE; iris family

Height/habit: Grassy clumps 1–1.5 ft. (30–45 cm.) high/wide.
Leaves: Flat swords, 1 in. (2.5 cm.) wide x 1–1.5 ft. (30–45 cm.) long; flowers occur at the tip of a leaflike spike that follows the production of 12 leaves in a fan.
Flowers: Irislike, fleeting, to 2 in. (5 cm.) across; white with touches of brown, blue, or yellow.
Season: Spring through summer; various seasons when grown as a houseplant.
When to plant: Set rhizomes in spring, barely covered with soil, 1 ft. (30 cm.) apart; set transplants when available. Hardy zone 9 and warmer.
Light: Sun to half shade.
Soil: Well drained, moist.
Fertilizer: 5-10-5, 14-14-14.
Storage: Store briefly in damp soil at 50–60°F (10–15°C); cut back the leaves to 4–5 in. (10–12.5 cm.) to reduce transpiration.
Propagation: Root offsets that form following flowering on each bloom stalk.
Uses: Beds, borders, pots, hanging baskets, houseplant.

NERINE
(neh-REYE-nee)
Guernsey Lily
AMARYLLIDACEAE; amaryllis
family

Height/habit: Grassy clumps,
1–1.5 ft. (30–45 cm.) high/wide.
Leaves: Narrow blades, 1–1.5 ft.
(30–45 cm.) long, appearing
before, during, or after flowers
bloom.
Flowers: Umbels atop a scape;
spidery, each 2–3 in. (5–7.5
cm.) across; pink, magenta,
red, rose, or scarlet.
Season: Fall.
When to plant: Set bulbs
2–4 in. (5–10 cm.) deep,
4–6 in. (10–15 cm.) apart in
late summer or early fall; set
transplants when available.
Ground-hardy zone 8 and
warmer.

Light: Sun half day or more.
Soil: Well drained; moist,
except on the dry side in
summer.
Fertilizer: 5-10-5.
Storage: Store bulbs in dry
peat moss at 50–60°F (10–15°C)
only from receipt until
planting time.
Propagation: Remove offsets
at planting time.
Uses: Beds, borders, pots,
cut flowers.

ORNITHOGALUM
(or-nith-OGG-al-um)
Chincherinchee;
Star-of-Bethlehem
LILIACEAE; lily family

Height/habit: Basal clumps
of grassy foliage with flowers
rising considerably above,
1–2 ft. (30–61 cm.).
Leaves: Thick, linear to lanceolate, 1–1.5 ft. (30–45 cm.) long.
Flowers: Racemes 1–1.5 ft.
(30–45 cm.) high bear many
fragrant flowers, each 1–2 in.
(2.5–5 cm.) wide; white.
Season: Spring through
summer.
When to plant: Set bulbs
2–4 in. (5–10 cm.) deep,
4–8 in. (10–20 cm.) apart in

fall. Ground-hardy zone 8
and warmer. Elsewhere can
be grown as a potted plant.
Light: Sun half day or more.
Soil: Well drained, moist.
Fertilizer: 5-10-5.
Storage: Store bulbs in dry
peat moss at 50–60°F (10–15°C)
from receipt until planting
time.
Propagation: Remove offsets
at planting time.
Uses: Beds, borders, pots,
outstanding cut flowers.

OXALIS
(OX-al-iss)

Lucky Clover; Wood Sorrel

OXALIDACEAE; oxalis family

Height/habit: Low, ground-covering plants, 3–6 in. (7.5–15 cm.).

Leaves: Small, to .5 in. (1.25 cm.); resemble clover, often with a contrasting zone of color.

Flowers: Delicate, shallow trumpets, each to 1 in. (2.5 cm.) across, in clusters atop a slender, wiry scape; red, pink, yellow, white, rose, or lavender.

Season: Spring through fall, depending on the species; winter in mild climates (zone 9 and warmer).

When to plant: Set bulbs or rhizomes 1–2 in. (2.5–5 cm.) deep, 4–6 in. (10–15 cm.) apart in fall or spring; transplants when available. Wild, weedy oxalis grows almost everywhere. Cultivated sorts are showier and ground-hardy zone 8 and warmer.

Light: Sun to half shade.

Soil: Well drained; moist, except dryness acceptable during dormancy.

Fertilizer: 5-10-5.

Storage: Store in dry peat moss at 50–60°F (10–15°C) from receipt until planting time.

Propagation: Remove offsets at planting time.

Uses: Beds, borders, rock and wild gardens, pots, hanging baskets.

PANCRATIUM
(pan-CRAY-shum)

Sea Daffodil

AMARYLLIDACEAE; amaryllis family

Height/habit: Basal foliage rosettes topped by umbels, to 3 ft. (1 m.).
Leaves: Evergreen, linear, to 2.5 ft. (76 cm.) long.
Flowers: Resemble daffodils but more spidery, to 3 in. (7.5 cm.) across; white; fragrant.
Season: Summer.
When to plant: Set bulbs 4–6 in. (10–15 cm.) deep, 6–8 in. (15–20 cm.) apart in fall or spring; transplants when available. Ground-hardy zone 8 and warmer; elsewhere dig and bring inside before hard freezing in the fall, or grow as a container plant.
Light: Sun half day or more.
Soil: Humusy, well drained; moist, except on the dry side fall through winter.
Fertilizer: 5-10-5.
Storage: Store bulbs in dry peat moss at 50–60°F (10–15°C) from receipt until planting time.
Propagation: Remove offsets in spring.
Uses: Beds, borders, pots, cut flowers.

PLEIONE
(ply-OH-nee)

Indian Crocus

ORCHIDACEAE; orchid family

Height/habit: Small orchid, to
8 in. (20 cm.).
Leaves: Plicate (fanlike), lance-
shaped, 4–8 in. (10–20 cm.)
long.
Flowers: Resemble a small,
showy cattleya orchid, to 3 in.
(7.5 cm.) across; lavender pink,
rose, white, or yellow.
Season: Spring.
When to plant: Set transplants
when available for outdoor
gardens zone 10 and warmer.
Elsewhere, pleiones need to be
brought indoors at the first

hint of freezing weather.
(There is always a large exhibit
of pleiones at the Chelsea
Flower Show in London, held
annually during the third week
of May.)
Light: Sun to half shade.
Soil: Use a purchased mix
labeled for epiphytic orchids.
Pot in a shallow pan with special drainage cuts.
Fertilizer: 14-14-14.
Storage: Quite cool (40–50°F
[4–10°C]) and on the dry side
in fall through winter, but
not to the point of freezing in
their pots.
Propagation: Remove offsets
in spring.
Uses: Mostly in pots.

POLIANTHES
(polly-ANTH-eez)

Mexican Tuberose

AGAVACEAE; agave family

Height/habit: Basal rosettes from which rise the tall spikes of flowers, to 2.5 ft. (76 cm.).

Leaves: Succulent, grassy, each to 1.5 ft. (45 cm.) long.

Flowers: Single or double, each 1–2 in. (2.5–5 cm.) across, growing from spikes; fragrant; white with touches of pink, especially in the double-flowered variety.

Season: Late summer through fall.

When to plant: Set the tuberous rootstock 2–4 in. (5–10 cm.) deep, 6–12 in. (15–30 cm.) apart in spring. Ground-hardy zone 9 and warmer. Elsewhere, dig before fall killing frost and place in a protected place. Single-flowered species naturalize better in mild-climate gardens than do the doubles.

Light: Sun half day or more.

Soil: Well drained; moist, except dry during winter dormancy.

Fertilizer: 5-10-5.

Storage: Store in dry peat moss at 50–60°F (10–15°C) from fall to winter until planting time.

Propagation: Remove offsets at planting time. For best results, however, leave each rootstock intact from year to year.

Uses: Beds, borders, pots, cut flowers.

PUSCHKINIA
(push-KIN-ee-ah)

Striped Squill

LILIACEAE; lily family

Height/habit: Basal rosettes grow upright, to 6 in. (15 cm.).
Leaves: Strap-shaped, linear, to 6 in. (15 cm.) long.
Flowers: Short spikes, bell-like, each to 1 in. (2.5 cm.) across; porcelain blue often with greenish stripe.
Season: Spring.
When to plant: Set bulbs 2–4 in. (5–10 cm.) deep, 4–6 in. (10–15 cm.) apart in fall.

Ground-hardy zone 4 and warmer but not reliable for return seasons zone 8 and warmer.
Light: Sun to half shade.
Soil: Well drained; moist, except summer dryness acceptable.
Fertilizer: 5-10-5.
Storage: Store bulbs in dry peat moss at 40–50°F (4–10°C) from receipt until planting time.
Propagation: Remove offsets at planting time.
Uses: Beds, borders, pots.

RANUNCULUS
(rah-NUNK-yew-lus)

Buttercup

RANUNCULACEAE; buttercup family

Height/habit: Basal foliage resembling parsley, above which the flowers appear, to 15 in. (38 cm.).
Leaves: Dissected, cut, 8–10 in. (20–25 cm.) long/wide.
Flowers: Double, many rounded, overlapping petals, 2–3 in. (5–7.5 cm.) across; most colors except blue.
Season: Spring.
When to plant: Set tubers 2–4 in. (5–10 cm.) deep, 4–6 in. (10–15 cm.) apart in fall (spring zone 7 and colder).
Light: Sun half day or more.
Soil: Well drained, moist.
Fertilizer: 5-10-5.
Storage: Place tubers in dry peat moss at 50–60°F (10–15°C) from receipt until planting time. They sprout more quickly if soaked 24 hours in water at room temperature immediately before planting.
Propagation: Divide at planting time.
Uses: Beds, borders, cut flowers.

RHODOHYPOXIS
(rho-doh-high-POX-iss)

Red Star

HYPOXIDACEAE; hypoxis family

Height/habit: Short, grasslike plants from a rhizome with fleshy roots, 3–4 in. (7.5–10 cm.) high/wide.
Leaves: Basal, 3–4 in. (7.5–10 cm.) long; ribbed with silky hairs.
Flowers: Starry, 6–petaled, to 1 in. (2.5 cm.) across; white, rose, pink, or crimson.
Season: Spring through early summer.
When to plant: Set transplants when available; rhizomes 1 in. (2.5 cm.) deep, 3 in. (7.5 cm.) apart in fall. Ground-hardy zone 8 and warmer.
Light: Sun to half sun.
Soil: Well drained, moist.
Fertilizer: 5-10-5.
Storage: Store bulbs in dry peat moss at 40–50°F (4–10°C), as briefly as possible, from receipt until planting time.
Propagation: Divide or sow seeds in spring.
Uses: Rock garden or pots.

SCADOXUS
(skad-OX-us)
Blood Lily
AMARYLLIDACEAE; amaryllis
family

Height/habit: A red-spotted
stalk rises from each bulb to
6–8 in. (15–20 cm.), at which
point the leaves unfurl, causing
the plant to reach 1–1.5 ft.
(30–45 cm.).
Leaves: Rounded, lanceolate,
6–10 in. (15–25 cm.) long.
Flowers: Appear in a ball in
groups of up to 100, each to
1 in. (2.5 cm.) across, atop a
stiff scape; coral pink, salmon,
or crimson; sometimes
known as *Haemanthus.*
Season: Spring through
summer.
When to plant: Set bulbs 2 in.
(5 cm.) deep, 6–12 in. (15–30
cm.) apart at the beginning of
warm weather; set transplants
in pots as available. Ground-
hardy zone 9 and warmer.
Light: Sun to half sun.
Soil: Well drained, moist,
except quite dry during winter
dormancy.
Fertilizer: 5-10-5.
Storage: Store bulbs in dry
peat moss at 50–60°F (10–15°C)
from fall through winter until
planting time.
Propagation: Remove offsets
at planting time.
Uses: Beds, borders, pots,
cut flowers.

SCHIZOSTYLIS
(sky-zoh-STYLE-iss)

Crimson Flag; River Lily

IRIDACEAE; iris family

Height/habit: Grassy evergreen clumps 2–2.5 ft. (61–76 cm.) high/wide.

Leaves: Sword-shaped, narrow, 12–15 in. (30–38 cm.) long.

Flowers: Slender stalks bear 6–14 starry blossoms to 2 in. (5 cm.) across; scarlet red.

Season: Summer through fall.

When to plant: Set rhizomes 1 in. (2.5 cm.) deep, 8–12 in. (20–30 cm.) apart in spring; set transplants when available. Ground-hardy zone 9 and warmer; elsewhere, grow in containers or dig before frost and winter as for gladiolus.

Light: Sun half day or more.

Soil: Well drained, moist.

Fertilizer: 5-10-5.

Storage: Store bulbs in dry peat moss at 50°F (10°C), as briefly as possible, from receipt until planting time.

Propagation: Divide or sow seeds spring or fall.

Uses: Beds, borders, pots.

SCILLA
(SILL-ah)
Squill
LILIACEAE; lily family

Height/habit: Fleshy foliage from the base, 6–12 in. (15–30 cm.) high/wide.
Leaves: To 6 in. (15 cm.) long, grasslike in some species.
Flowers: Nodding bells or dense clusters of stars, each to 1 in. (2.5 cm.) across; blue, dark purplish blue, or lavender.
Season: Early spring.
When to plant: Set bulbs 2–4 in. (5–10 cm.) deep, 4–8 in. (10–20 cm.) apart in the fall. Siberian squill (*S. siberica*) ground-hardy zone 4 and warmer but might not return after the first season zone 9 and warmer. Peruvian squill (*S. peruviana*), also called Cuban lily, is ground-hardy zone 9 and warmer and makes a fine pot specimen.
Light: Sun half day or more.
Soil: Well drained; moist, except summer dryness acceptable.
Fertilizer: 5-10-5.
Storage: Store bulbs in dry peat moss at 40–50°F (4–10°C) from receipt until planting time.
Propagation: Remove offsets at planting time.
Uses: Beds, borders, ground cover, pots, cut flowers.

SEEMANNIA
(see-MANN-ee-ah)
Seemannia
GESNERIACEAE; gesneriad family

Height/habit: Upright, bushy, 1.5–2.5 ft. (45–76 cm.) high/wide.
Leaves: Lightly covered with hairs, lance-shaped, 2–3 in. (5–7.5 cm.) long.
Flowers: Tubular, about 1 in. (2.5 cm.) long; bloom in great profusion; orange-red.
Season: Warm weather or any season in a warm greenhouse.
When to plant: Set scaly rhizomes 1–2 in. (2.5–5 cm.) deep, 4–6 in. (10–15 cm.) apart at the beginning of warm growing season. Ground-hardy zone 10 and warmer.
Light: Half sun to half shade.
Soil: Humusy, well drained, moist.
Fertilizer: 5-10-5.
Storage: Store scaly rhizomes in dry peat moss at 50–60°F (10–15°C) from fall through winter until planting time.
Propagation: Break up larger rhizomes at planting time.
Uses: Beds, borders, pots.

Florists' Gloxinia

GESNERIACEAE; gesneriad family

Height/habit: Compact rosettes of foliage surrounding large numbers of flowers that grow from the center, to about 4 in. (10 cm.).

Leaves: Succulent, hairy, veined, and quilted, 6–12 in. (15–30 cm.) long/wide.

Flowers: Upright or outward-facing, single or double, 1–4 in. (2.5–10 cm.) across; some fragrant; most colors except yellow and orange.

Season: When outdoor weather is warm or at almost any time in a warm greenhouse or indoor fluorescent-light garden.

When to plant: Set tubers rounded side down, hollowed-out side up, not more than 1 in. (2.5 cm.) deep, 1 ft. (30 cm.) apart at the beginning of a warm growing season. Hardy outdoors zone 10 and warmer; elsewhere, tubers must be brought inside when there is danger of frost.

Light: Half sun to half shade. Ideal porch plants where there is bright, indirect light and protection from rain and wind.

Soil: Humusy, well drained; moist, except quite dry during the season of rest (usually fall through winter).

Fertilizer: 5-10-5.

Storage: Store tubers in dry peat moss at about 60°F (15°C) from fall through winter until planting time.

Propagation: Divide tubers at planting time; alternatively, sow seeds or take leaf cuttings.

Uses: Beds, borders, pots. There are miniatures, such as *S. pusilla*, that thrive in a terrarium or bubble bowl.

SMITHIANTHA
(smith-ee-ANTH-ah)

Temple Bells

GESNERIACEAE; gesneriad family

Height/habit: Upright, 2–3 ft. (61–90 cm.) high/wide.

Leaves: Densely haired, crenate, heart-shaped, to 4–5 in. (10–12.5 cm.) across; often marbled reddish brown.

Flowers: Nodding or outward-facing tubular bells, each to 1 in. (2.5 cm.) across; bloom in great numbers; yellow, orange-red.

Season: Summer or at almost any time in a warm, humid indoor garden.

When to plant: Set scaly rhizomes 2 in. (5 cm.) deep, 4–8 in. (10–20 cm.) apart at the beginning of warm weather. Ground-hardy zone 10 and warmer.

Light: Half sun to half shade.

Soil: Humusy, well drained, moist.

Fertilizer: 5-10-5.

Storage: Store scaly rhizomes in dry peat moss at 50–60°F (10–15°C) from fall through winter until planting time.

Propagation: Break apart large scaly rhizomes at planting time.

Uses: Beds, borders, pots.

Wandflower; Velvet Flower

IRIDACEAE; iris family

Height/habit: Grassy clumps, to 1 ft. (30 cm.) high/wide.

Leaves: Narrow swords in 2 ranks along the stem, to 1 ft. (30 cm.) long.

Flowers: Several along a wiry stalk, each to 2 in. (5 cm.) across; vivid colors and combinations, including yellow, scarlet, purplish black, orange, and crimson.

Season: Spring.

When to plant: Set corms 3–4 in. (7.5–10 cm.) deep, 4–8 in. (10–20 cm.) apart in fall (mild climates) or in spring zone 6 and colder.

Light: Sun half day or more.

Soil: Well drained, moist, except quite dry during summer rest.

Fertilizer: 5-10-5.

Storage: Store corms in dry peat moss at 50–60°F (10–15°C) from receipt until planting time.

Propagation: Remove offsets at planting time or sow seeds.

Uses: Beds, borders, pots, cut flowers.

SPREKELIA
(spreh-KEE-lee-ah)

Jacobean Lily; Aztec Lily

AMARYLLIDACEAE; amaryllis family

Height/habit: Grassy clumps to 12–15 in. (30–38 cm.) high/wide.

Leaves: Narrow, linear, to 1 ft. (30 cm.) long, appearing after the flowers.

Flowers: 1 per 1-foot- (30-cm-) long stalk, to 5 in. (12.5 cm.) across; intense crimson.

Season: Early summer.

When to plant: Set bulbs 2–4 in. (5–10 cm.) deep, 4–8 in. (10–20 cm.) apart in spring. Ground-hardy zone 9 and warmer; elsewhere, treat as gladiolus. Rather notorious for not blooming after the first season.

Light: Sun half day or more.

Soil: Well drained, moist, except quite dry fall through winter.

Fertilizer: 5-10-5.

Storage: Store bulbs in dry peat moss at 50–60°F (10–15°C) from fall through winter until planting time.

Propagation: Remove offsets at planting time or sow seeds.

Uses: Beds, borders, pots, cut flowers.

STERNBERGIA
(stern-BERJ-ee-ah)

Winter Daffodil; Lily of the Field

AMARYLLIDACEAE; amaryllis family

Height/habit: Grassy clumps, to 1 ft. (30 cm.) high/wide.
Leaves: Narrow, linear, to 1 ft. (30 cm.) long.
Flowers: Crocuslike, to 2 in. (5 cm.) across; bright golden yellow.
Season: Fall.
When to plant: Set bulbs 4 in. (10 cm.) deep, 8–12 in. (20–30 cm.) apart in late summer. Ground-hardy zone 7 and warmer, zone 6 if protected.

Light: Sun half day or more.
Soil: Well drained; moist, except summer dryness acceptable.
Fertilizer: 5-10-5.
Storage: Store bulbs in dry peat moss at 50–60°F (10–15°C) from receipt until planting time.
Propagation: Remove offsets at planting time or sow seeds. Excellent colonizer in many situations.
Uses: Beds, borders, rock gardens, pots.

TACCA
(TACK-ah)

Batflower

TACCACEAE; tacca family

Height/habit: Leafy clumps to 2 ft. (61 cm.) high/wide.
Leaves: Olive green, quilted, 1.5–2 ft. (20–61 cm.) long.
Flowers: Curiously batlike, 4–6 in. (10–15 cm.) across, with a spreading bract and long, whiskerlike filaments; maroon to black.
Season: Spring through summer; any season in a warm, humid greenhouse.
When to plant: Set transplants when available. Root-hardy zone 10 and warmer; elsewhere, treat as a container plant that can be moved indoors when temperatures drop below 50°F (10°C).
Light: Half sun to half shade.
Soil: Humusy, well drained, moist.
Fertilizer: 5-10-5.
Storage: Rest rootstock in dry peat moss at 50–60°F (10–15°C) from fall through winter until planting time.
Propagation: Remove offsets in spring.
Uses: Beds, borders, pots.

TIGRIDIA
(teye-GRID-ee-ah)

Mexican Shellflower

IRIDACEAE; iris family

Height/habit: Upright leaves above which the flowers appear, rising to 1.5–2 ft. (20–61 cm.).

Leaves: Ribbed, narrow swords, 8–12 in. (20–30 cm.) long, on erect stems rising from corms.

Flowers: Last only for 1 day. Cupped with spreading segments in groups of 3, to 3 in. (7.5 cm.) across; brilliant yellows, oranges, pinks, or reds with contrasting spots.

Season: Late spring through summer.

When to plant: Set corms 4–6 in. (10–15 cm.) deep, 6–8 in. (15–20 cm.) apart in spring. Ground-hardy zone 9 and warmer.

Light: Sun half day or more.

Soil: Well drained, moist.

Fertilizer: 5-10-5.

Storage: Store corms in dry peat moss at 50–60°F (10–15°C) from fall through winter until planting time.

Propagation: Plant cormlets separately or sow seeds for blooms the next season in spring.

Uses: Beds, borders, pots.

TRITONIA
(try-TOH-nee-ah)
Montbretia; Flame Freesia
IRIDACEAE; iris family

Height/habit: Grassy clumps with flowers hovering above, 1–1.5 ft. (30–45 cm.) high/wide.
Leaves: Narrow swords, to 1.5 ft. (45 cm.).
Flowers: Bell- to cup-shaped, each 1–2 in. (2.5–5 cm.) across, on wiry stems; yellow, orange, or coral.
Season: Fall, winter, spring, early summer, depending on planting time and local temperatures.
When to plant: Set corms 2–4 in. (5–10 cm.) deep, 4–8 in. (10–20 cm.) apart when available; fall in mild climates, spring in colder regions. Ground-hardy zone 9 and warmer.

Light: Sun half day or more.
Soil: Well drained; moist, except summer dryness acceptable.
Fertilizer: 5-10-5.
Storage: Store corms in dry peat moss at 40–50°F (4–10°C) from receipt until planting time.
Propagation: Separate clumps at beginning of growing season.
Uses: Beds, borders, pots, cut flowers.

TROPAEOLUM
(tropp-ee-OH-lum)
Tuber Nasturtiums
TROPAEOLACEAE; nasturtium family

Height/habit: *T. tuberosum* and *T. tricolorum* are climbers, 5–15 ft. (1.5–4.5 m.).
Leaves: Rounded, 5- or 6-lobed, to 1 in. (2.5 cm.) across, on wiry stems.
Flowers: Tubular, to 1 in. (2.5 cm.) long; scarlet, purple, red, or yellow.
Season: Spring through summer.
When to plant: Set tubers 1–2 in. (2.5–5 cm.) deep, 1 ft. (30 cm.) apart in spring. Ground-hardy zone 8 and warmer.

Light: Sun half day or more.
Soil: Well drained, moist.
Fertilizer: 5-10-5.
Storage: Store tubers in dry peat moss at 50–60°F (10–15°C) from fall through winter until planting time.
Propagation: Divide at planting time.
Uses: Trailing over shrubbery or brush, on small trellis or tepee, spilling from hanging baskets.

TULBAGHIA
(tull-BAY-ghee-ah)

Society Garlic

AMARYLLIDACEAE; amaryllis family

Height/habit: Grassy clumps, 1–1.5 ft. (30–45 cm.) high/wide.
Leaves: Linear, glaucous, to 1 ft. (30 cm.) long. Variegated lengthwise in *T. violacea* 'Tricolor,' which is green, cream, and bronze.
Flowers: Umbels of 20–40, each to 1 in. (2.5 cm.) across, atop a slender scape to 2 ft. (61 cm.) long; fragrant in *T. fragrans* but somewhat overpowered by the oniony smell of the plant itself; lilac to lavender purple.

Season: Spring through summer through fall.
When to plant: Set transplants when available, ideally in spring. Ground-hardy zone 9 and warmer.
Light: Sun half day or more.
Soil: Well drained; moist, except summer dryness acceptable.
Fertilizer: 5-10-5.
Storage: Store bulbs in dry peat moss at 50–60°F (10–15°C) from receipt until planting time.
Propagation: Divide or sow seeds in spring.
Uses: Beds, borders, pots, cut flowers.

TULIPA
(TEW-lip-ah)
Tulip
LILIACEAE; lily family

Height/habit: Upright, 4–36 in.
(10–90 cm.).
Leaves: Glaucous, succulent,
grassy to wide, 4–12 in.
(10–30 cm.) long x .5–4 in.
(1.25–10 cm.) wide.
Flowers: Single or double,
1–8 in. (2.5–20 cm.) wide; all
colors between (and including)
white and black.
Season: Spring.
When to plant: Set bulbs
4–8 in. (10–20 cm.) deep,
6–10 in. (15–25 cm.) apart
in fall zone 8 and warmer.
Ground-hardy just about
everywhere but not depend-
able for repeat bloom
zone 8 and warmer.
Light: Sun half day or more.
Soil: Well drained; moist,
except summer dryness
desirable.
Fertilizer: 5-10-5.
Storage: Store bulbs in dry
peat moss at 40–50°F (4–10°C)
until planting time. For zone 8
and warmer, it is common
practice to refrigerate (not
freeze) tulip bulbs from the
time they arrive in the fall
until planting the last week
of December.
Propagation: Remove offsets
at planting time or sow seeds
(not practical except in cold
temperate regions, basically
zone 6 and colder).
Uses: Beds, borders, pots,
cut flowers.

VALLOTA
(val-LOT-ah)

Scarborough Lily

AMARYLLIDACEAE; amaryllis
family

Height/habit: Clumps of
evergreen leaves, 1.5–2 ft.
(20–61 cm.) high/wide.
Leaves: Strap-shaped, 1–1.5 ft.
(30–45 cm.) long, reddish at
the edges and on the under-
sides.
Flowers: Funnel-shaped, to
3-in. (7.5 cm.) across, in a
cluster at the top of a hollow
stalk the size of a pencil; scarlet.
Season: Summer through fall.
When to plant: Set bulbs with
the neck and some shoulder
above the soil, 6–12 in. (15–30
cm.) apart at any season; set
transplants when available.

Hardy zone 10 and warmer,
elsewhere grow as a container
plant and bring inside when
frost threatens.
Light: Sun half day or more.
Soil: Humusy, well drained,
moist; avoid severe drying
even during the cool winter
rest.
Fertilizer: 5-10-5.
Storage: Store bulbs in dry
peat moss at 50°F (10°C), as
briefly as possible, from receipt
until planting time.
Propagation: Remove offsets
at planting time, but note:
Established, undisturbed bulbs
produce the most flowers.
Uses: Beds, borders, pots,
cut flowers.

VELTHEIMIA
(vel-THEEM-ee-ah)

Forest Lily

LILIACEAE; lily family

Height/habit: Showy flowers
rise from basal foliage rosette,
to about 2 ft (61 cm.).
Leaves: Wavy-margined,
somewhat succulent, 6–8 in.
(15–20 cm.) long x 2 in.
(5 cm.) wide.
Flowers: Tubular, nodding,
1–2 in. (2.5–5 cm.) long,
clustered symmetrically at the
top of a sturdy stalk; chartreuse
to pink and dusty red, often
green-tipped.
Season: Winter or spring.
When to plant: Set bulbs in
fall, the tips just exposed,
8–12 in. (20–30 cm.) apart.

Ground-hardy zone 9 and
warmer; elsewhere grow as
a container plant and protect
from freezing. A cool start-up
season fall through winter
leads to a perfect flower show
winter through early spring.
Light: Sun half day or more.
Soil: Well drained, moist,
except dry in summer during
dormancy.
Fertilizer: 5-10-5.
Storage: Store bulbs in dry
peat moss at 50–60°F (10–15°C)
from receipt until planting
time.
Propagation: Remove offsets
at planting time or sow seeds.
Uses: Beds, borders, pots,
cut flowers.

ZANTEDESCHIA
(zant-eh-DEE-shuh)

Calla Lily

ARACEAE; aroid family

Height/habit: Upright in clumps, 1–3 ft. (30–90 cm.) high/wide.

Leaves: Arrowhead- or lance-shaped, 6–8 in. (15–20 cm.) long, to half as wide; spotted translucent white in some.

Flowers: Curving, petal-like spathe, 2–8 in. (5–20 cm.) long; white, yellow, pink, rose, or apricot.

Season: Winter through spring for white callas; often spring through summer for the yellows and pastels.

When to plant: Set white tubers late summer through early fall, the others winter through spring, 2 in. (5 cm.) deep, 4–6 in. (10–15 cm.) apart. Maintain warm to moist conditions thereafter. Ground-hardy zone 9 and south; else-where, grow in pots or dig and bring inside before hard frost.

Light: Half sun to half shade.

Soil: Well drained, moist to wet. While growing actively a pot of callas can be left standing in a saucer of water.

Fertilizer: 5-10-5, 14-14-14.

Storage: Store tubers in dry peat moss at 50–60°F (10–15°C) from receipt until planting time.

Propagation: Divide at beginning of growing season or sow seeds.

Uses: Beds, borders, pots, cut flowers.

ZEPHYRANTHES
(zeff-er-ANTH-eez)
Rain Lily
AMARYLLIDACEAE; amaryllis
family

Height/habit: Grassy clumps,
6–18 in. (15–45 cm.) high/wide.
Leaves: Evergreen or
deciduous; narrow, some
thin as coarse grass, 6–18 in.
(15–45 cm.) long.
Flowers: Funnel-shaped,
1–3 in. (2.5–7.5 cm.) across;
white, yellow, pink, or rose.
Season: Summer through
fall, mostly in response to
signficant rainfall, as common
name implies.
When to plant: Set bulbs
2–4 in. (5–10 cm.) deep, 4–8 in.
(10–20 cm.) apart in spring.
Use transplants when available. They are easy to dig and
replant. Ground-hardy zone 7
and warmer, especially popu-
lar along the Gulf Coast.
Light: Sun to half shade.
Soil: Well drained; moist to on
the dry side.
Fertilizer: 5-10-5.
Storage: Store bulbs briefly
in dry peat moss at 50–60°F
(10–15°C), from receipt until
planting time.
Propagation: Remove offsets
or sow seeds from spring
through summer.
Uses: Beds, borders, rock and
wild gardens, pots.

ZINGIBER
(ZING-ib-er)

Ginger

ZINGIBERACEAE; ginger family

Height/habit: Upright rhizomatous perennial, to 3 ft. (1 m.).

Leaves: To 1 ft. (30 cm.) long x 1–2 in. (2.5–5 cm.) wide; smell strongly of ginger when disturbed.

Flowers: Dense cone-shaped spikes to 3 in. (7.5 cm.) long; yellowish green spotted yellow.

Season: Summer until cold weather.

When to plant: Set rhizome rootstocks 2–4 in. (5–10 cm.) deep, 6–12 in. (20–30 cm.) apart in spring; or set transplants at the beginning of warm weather. Ground-hardy zone 9 and warmer; elsewhere, maintain as large container plants.

Light: Half sun to half shade.

Soil: Humusy, well drained, moist.

Fertilizer: 5-10-5, 14-14-14.

Storage: Store tuberous roots in dry peat moss at 50–60°F (10–15°C) from receipt until planting time.

Propagation: Divide tuberous roots in spring.

Uses: Beds, borders, ground cover in part shade, pots.

Chapter Three
Troubleshooting Guide for Bulbs

*S*ubjected to being in storage and living in the garden for many years, bulbs undergo a great deal. Sometimes, things go awry. Here are common problems and advice for how to handle them.

Bulb shriveled up and dry or soggy and possibly foul smelling.

Indicates the bulb has succumbed to some extreme stress such as freezing or overheating, drying, or waterlogging. Discard.

Little green bugs clustered on new shoots, especially flower buds.

Indicates aphids, also known as plant lice. Rub off with fingers or wash away with water sprays. Usually not serious.

Bulbs have been in garden for several years. Originally they bloomed, now there are few if any flowers.

Indicates a need for digging, dividing, and resetting the bulbs. Before doing any of this, refurbish the soil by adding up to 6 inches (15 centimeters) of well-rotted compost and a dusting of organic fertilizer, then till or fork together with the endemic soil.

Summer bulbs planted in the spring have grown spindly leaves on weak stems; there are no flowers.

This indicates planting in poorly prepared soil and in a site that is too shaded. With a few exceptions, such as the gingers, bulbs need four hours or more of sunlight a day during the time of year when they put most of their energies into growing.

Bulbs have lots of healthy leaves but no flowers.

This may indicate a too rich soil or an excess of nitrogen. Apply a fertilizer labeled specifically for flowering plants, 15-30-15 for example. This could also indicate that spring bulbs in pots have been forced in temperatures too warm, thus preventing the flower buds from developing.

Bulb foliage streaked with yellow, progresses slowly, then collapses.

This indicates a bulb that has disintegrated from one or more stresses, such as overheating while in transit or after it was planted. Conversely, the planting might have been over- or under-watered at a critical stage.

Chapter Four
Bringing Bulbs Into Your Home

Bulbs provide some of the flower world's loveliest and most fragrant blooms. One of their nicest attributes is that gardeners can bring them indoors to bloom in pots weeks or months ahead of their normal appearance outdoors, a process known as forcing.

One of the most common methods of forcing involves containers with drainage holes. Partially fill the pot with soil. Place the bulb on top, pointed (nose) side up so that they're just about even with the rim. Then add soil until it almost covers the bulbs. Water well and keep soil moist. Place in the refrigerator, a root cellar, or an outdoor cold frame (covered with mulch). The temperature must be about 40–50° F (4–10°C). After about twelve to fifteen weeks, bring them into the house to bloom, preferably in indirect sunlight. You can stagger the process to have bulbs throughout the bleakest times of winter.

Gardeners can also force some bulbs in containers without drainage holes. 'Paperwhite' narcissi are good candidates, available in several look-alike cultivars that in their natural order bloom early, midseason, and late, thus making it possible to have fresh, fragrant indoor blooms from about October until March. To do so, place 1–2 in. (2.5–5 cm.) of gravel in a low container. Add bulbs, pointed side up, and anchor with a little more gravel. Add water. They will bloom at room temperature (60–65°F [15–18°C] is ideal). Keep them in a window until the time they are about to flower.

Hydroponic forcing is another easy method that involves chilling the plants in a cellar or in the refrigerator as noted previously. Dutch and Roman hyacinths respond well to this treatment. They look lovely grown in specially shaped hyacinth glasses, which cradle each bulb so that water reaches only the base. If this container is clear, you can observe the emergence and growth of the white roots. Aside from hyacinth glasses, small pilsner glasses work well for hydroponic forcing.

Of course, you can always bring in bulb arrangements from the garden. Here are some suggestions, mixing in other types of plants from the home plot and the florist:

- Snowdrops with early-blooming tulips
- Iris with poppies and anemones
- Star-of-Bethlehem with gerbera daisies
- Iris, kangaroo paw, Kaffir lily, or agapanthus in ikebana arrangements
- Freesia or lily of the valley with miniature roses
- Gladioli and dahlias
- Anemones with brodiaea.

For everlastings arrangements and potpourri, the following air-dried flowers and seed heads are recommended:

- Alliums with gladiolus leaves
- Ranunculus, roses, and poppy seed heads
- Daffodil petals for bright potpourri color
- Grape hyacinth blossoms for subtle scent in potpourri
- Iris blossoms for light violet scent and color in potpourri
- Whole lily flowers as elegant topping for potpourri

Bibliography

Bailey, Liberty Hyde, and Ethel Zoe Bailey; revised and expanded by the staff of the L.H. Bailey Hortorium. 1976. *Hortus Third.* New York: Macmillan Publishing Co.

Bailey, Ralph; McDonald, Elvin; Good Housekeeping Editors. 1972. *The Good Housekeeping Illustrated Encyclopedia of Gardening.* New York: Book Division, Hearst Magazines.

Graf, Alfred Byrd. 1992. *Hortica.* New Jersey: Roehrs Co.

Greenlee, John. 1992. *The Encyclopedia of Ornamental Grasses.* Pennsylvania: Rodale Press.

Heriteau, Jacqueline, and Charles B. Thomas. 1994. *Water Gardens.* Boston/New York: Houghton Mifflin Co.

Hobhouse, Penelope, and Elvin McDonald, Consulting Editors. 1994. *Gardens of the World: The Art & Practice of Gardening.* New York: Macmillan Publishing Co.

Hobhouse, Penelope. 1994. *On Gardening.* New York: Macmillan Publishing Co.

McDonald, Elvin. 1993. *The New Houseplant: Bringing the Garden Indoors.* New York: Macmillan Publishing Co.

McDonald, Elvin. 1995. *The Color Garden Series: Red, White, Blue, Yellow.* San Francisco: Collins Publishers.

McDonald, Elvin. 1995. *The Traditional Home Book of Roses.* Des Moines: Meredith Books.

Mulligan, William C. 1992. *The Adventurous Gardener's Sourcebook of Rare and Unusual Plants.* New York: Simon & Schuster.

Mulligan, William C. 1995. *The Lattice Gardener.* New York: Macmillan Publishing Co.

River Oaks Garden Club. 1989. Fourth Revised Edition. *A Garden Book for Houston.* Houston: Gulf Publishing Co.

Royal Horticultural Society, The; Clayton, John, revised by John Main. Third Edition. 1992. *Pruning Ornamental Shrubs.* London: Cassell Educational Ltd.

Scanniello, Stephen, and Tania Bayard. 1994 *Climbing Roses.* New York: Prentice Hall.

Schinz, Marina, and Gabrielle van Zuylen. 1991. *The Gardens of Russell Page.* New York: Stewart, Tabori & Chang.

Sedenko, Jerry. 1991. *The Butterfly Garden.* New York: Villard Books.

Sunset Books and Sunset Magazine. 1995. *Sunset Western Garden Book.* Menlo Park: Sunset Publishing Co.

Woods, Christopher. 1992. *Encyclopedia of Perennials.* New York: Facts On File, Inc.

Yang, Linda. 1995. *The City & Town Gardener: A Handbook for Planting Small Spaces and Containers.* New York: Random House.

Resources

Jacques Amand
P.O. Box 59001
Potomac, MD 20859
free catalog; all kinds of bulbs

Amaryllis, Inc.
P.O. Box 318
Baton Rouge, LA 70821
free list; hybrid Hippeastrum

Antique Rose Emporium
Rt. 5, Box 143
Brenham, TX 77833
catalog $5; old roses, also perennials, ornamental grasses

Appalachian Gardens
Box 82
Waynesboro, PA 17268
catalog $2; uncommon woodies

B & D Lilies
330 "P" St.
Port Townsend, WA 98368
catalog $3; garden lilies

The Banana Tree, Inc.
715 Northampton St.
Easton, PA 18042
catalog $3; seeds of exotics

Beaver Creek Nursery
7526 Pelleaux Rd.
Knoxville, TN 37938
catalog $1; uncommon woodies

Kurt Bluemel
2740 Greene Lane
Baldwin, MD 21013
catalog $2; ornamental grasses, perennials

Bluestone Perennials
7237 Middle Ridge
Madison, OH 44057
free catalog; perennials

Borboleta Gardens
15980 Canby Ave., Rt. 5
Faribault, MN 55021
catalog $3; bulbs, tubers, corms, rhizomes

Bovees Nursery
1737 S.W. Coronado
Portland, OR 97219
catalog $2; uncommon woodies

Brand Peony Farms
P.O. Box 842
St. Cloud, MN 56302
free catalog; peonies

Breck's
6523 N. Galena Rd.
Peoria, IL 61632
free catalog; all kinds of bulbs

Briarwood Gardens
14 Gully Lane, R.F.D. 1
East Sandwich, MA 02537
list $1; azaleas, rhododendrons

Brudy's Tropical Exotics
P.O. Box 820874
Houston, TX 77282
catalog $2; seeds, plants of exotics

W. Atlee Burpee Co.
300 Park Ave.
Warminster, PA 18974
free catalog; seeds, plants, bulbs, supplies, wide selection

Busse Gardens
5873 Oliver Ave., S.W.
Cokato, MN 55321
catalog $2; perennials

Camellia Forest Nursery
125 Carolina Forest
Chapel Hill, NC 27516
list $1; uncommon woodies

Canyon Creek Nursery
3527 DIY Creek Rd.
Oroville, CA 95965
catalog $2; silver-leaved plants

Carroll Gardens
Box 310
Westminster, MD 21158
catalog $2; perennials, woodies, herbs

Coastal Gardens
4611 Socastee Blvd.
Myrtle Beach, SC 29575
catalog $3; perennials

The Cummins Garden
22 Robertsville Rd.
Marlboro, NJ 07746
catalog $2; azaleas, rhododendrons, woodies

The Daffodil Mart
Rt. 3, Box 794
Gloucester, VA 23061
list $1; Narcissus specialists, other bulbs

Daylily World
P.O. Box 1612
Sanford, FL 32772
catalog $5; all kinds of Hemerocallis

deJager Bulb Co.
Box 2010
So. Hamilton, MA 01982
free list; all kinds of bulbs

Tom Dodd's Rare Plants
9131 Holly St.
Semmes, AL 36575
list $1; trees, shrubs, extremely select

Far North Gardens
16785 Harrison Rd.
Livonia, MI 48154
catalog $2; primulas, other perennials

Flora Lan Nursery
9625 Northwest
Roy Forest Grove, OR 97116
free catalog; uncommon woodies

Forest Farm
990 Tetherow Rd.
Williams, OR 97544-9599
catalog $3; uncommon woodies in small sizes

Fox Hill Farm
P.O. Box 7
Parma, MI 49269
catalog $1; all kinds of herbs

Howard B. French
Box 565
Pittsfield, VT 05762
free catalog; bulbs

Gardens of the Blue Ridge
Box 10
Pineola, NC 28662
catalog $3; wildflowers and ferns

D. S. George Nurseries
2515 Penfield Rd.
Fairport, NY 14450
free catalog; clematis

Girard Nurseries
Box 428
Geneva, OH 44041
free catalog; uncommon
woodies

Glasshouse Works
Greenhouses
Church St., Box 97
Stewart, OH 45778
catalog $2; exotics for
containers

Gossler Farms Nursery
1200 Weaver Rd.
Springfield, OR 97477
list $2; uncommon
woodies

Greenlee Ornamental Grasses
301 E. Franklin Ave.
Pomona, CA 91766
catalog $5; native and
ornamental grasses

Greer Gardens
1280 Goodpasture Island Rd.
Eugene, OR 97401
catalog $3; uncommon
woodies, especially
Rhododendron

Grigsby Cactus Gardens
2354 Bella Vista Dr.
Vista, CA 92084
catalog $2; cacti and
other succulents

Growers Service Co.
10118 Crouse Rd.
Hartland, MI 48353
list $1; all kinds of bulbs

Heirloom Old Garden Roses
24062 N.E. Riverside Dr.
St. Paul, OR 97137
catalog $5; old garden, English,
and winter-hardy roses

Holbrook Farm and Nursery
Box 368
Fletcher, NC 28732
free catalog; woodies and
other select plants

J. L. Hudson, Seedsman
P.O. Box 1058
Redwood City, CA 94064
catalog $1; nonhybrid flowers,
vegetables

Jackson and Perkins
1 Rose Lane
Medford, OR 97501
free catalog; roses, perennials

Kartuz Greenhouses
1408 Sunset Dr.
Vista, CA 92083
catalog $2; exotics
for containers

Klehm Nursery
Rt. 5, Box 197 Penny Rd.
So. Barrington, IL 60010
catalog $5; peonies,
Hemerocallis, hostas,
perennials

M. & J. Kristick
155 Mockingbird Rd.
Wellsville, PA 17365
free catalog; conifers

Lamb Nurseries
Rt. 1, Box 460B
Long Beach, WA 98631
catalog $1; perennials

Las Pilitas Nursery
Star Rt., Box 23
Santa Margarita, CA 93453
catalog $6; California natives

Lauray of Salisbury
432 Undermountain Rd.
Rt. 41
Salisbury, CT 06068
catalog $2; exotics
for containers

Lilypons Water Gardens
6800 Lilypons Rd.
P.O. Box 10
Buckeystown, MD 21717
catalog $5; aquatics

Limerock Ornamental Grasses
R.D. 1, Box 111
Port Matilda, PA 16870
list $3

Logee's Greenhouses
141 North St.
Danielson, CT 06239
catalog $3; exotics for
containers

Louisiana Nursery
Rt. 7, Box 43
Opelousas, LA 70570
catalogs $3–$6;
uncommon woodies,
perennials

Lowe's Own Root Roses
6 Sheffield Rd.
Nashua, NH 03062
list $5; old roses

McClure & Zimmerman
Box 368
Friesland, WI 53935
free catalog; all kinds of bulbs

Mellinger's
2310 W. South Range Rd. North
Lima, OH 44452
free catalog; all kinds of plants

Merry Gardens
Upper Mechanic St., Box 595
Camden, ME 04843
catalog $2; herbs,
pelargoniums, cultivars
of Hedera helix

Milaeger's Gardens
4838 Douglas Ave.
Racine, WI 53402
catalog $1; perennials

Moore Miniature Roses
2519 E. Noble Ave.
Visalia, CA 93292
catalog $1; all kinds of
miniature roses

Niche Gardens
1111 Dawson Rd.
Chapel Hill, NC 27516
catalog $3; perennials

Nichols Garden Nursery
1190 N. Pacific Highway
Albany, OR 97321
free catalog; uncommon
edibles, flowers, herbs

Nor'East Miniature Roses
Box 307
Rowley, MA 01969
free catalog

North Carolina State University
Arboretum
Box 7609
Raleigh, NC 27695
Propagation guide for woody
plants and lists of plants in
the arboretum, $10; member-
ship permits participation in
worthy plant propagation
and dissemination.

Oakes Daylilies
8204 Monday Rd.
Corryton, TN 37721
free catalog; all kinds
of Hemerocallis

Geo. W. Park Seed Co.
Box 31
Greenwood, SC 29747
free catalog; all kinds of seeds,
plants, and bulbs

Plants of the Southwest
Agua Fria, Rt. 6,
Box 11A
Santa Fe, NM 87501
catalog $3.50

Roses of Yesterday and Today
802 Brown's Valley Rd.
Watsonville, CA 95076
catalog $3 third class,
$5 first; old roses

Roslyn Nursery
211 Burrs Lane
Dix Hills, NY 11746
catalog $3; woodies, perennials

John Scheepers, Inc.
P.O. Box 700
Bantam, CT 06750
free catalog; all kinds of bulbs

Seymour's Selected Seeds
P.O. Box 1346
Sussex, VA 23884-0346
free catalog; English
cottage garden seeds

Shady Oaks Nursery
112 10th Ave. S.E.
Waseca, MN 56093
catalog $2.50; hostas, ferns,
wildflowers, shrubs

Siskiyou Rare Plant Nursery
2825 Cummings Rd.
Medford, OR 97501
catalog $2; alpines

Anthony J. Skittone
1415 Eucalyptus
San Francisco, CA 94132
catalog $2; unusual bulbs,
especially from South Africa

Sonoma Horticultural Nursery
3970 Azalea Ave.
Sebastopol, CA 95472
catalog $2; azaleas,
rhododendrons

Spring Hill Nurseries
110 W. Elm St.
Tipp City, OH 45371
free catalog; perennials,
woodies, roses

Sunnybrook Farms Homestead
9448 Mayfield Rd.
Chesterland, OH 44026
catalog $2; perennials, herbs

Surry Gardens
P.O. Box 145
Surry, ME 04684
free list; perennials, vines,
grasses, wild garden

Terrapin Springs Nursery
Box 7454
Tifton, GA 31793
list $1; uncommon
woodies

Thompson & Morgan
Box 1308
Jackson, NJ 08527
free catalog; all kinds
of seeds

Transplant Nursery
1586 Parkertown Rd.
Lavonia, GA 30553
catalog $1; azaleas,
rhododendrons

Twombly Nursery, Inc.
163 Barn Hill Rd.
Monroe, CT 06468
list $4; uncommon
woodies

Van Engelen, Inc.
Stillbrook Farm
313 Maple St.
Litchfield, CT 06759
free catalog; all kinds
of bulbs

Andre Viette Farm & Nursery
Rt. 1, Box 16
Fishersville, VA 22939
catalog $3; perennials,
ornamental grasses

Washington Evergreen Nursery
Box 388
Leicester, NC 28748
catalog $2; conifers

Wayside Gardens
One Garden Lane
Hodges, SC 29695
free catalog; all kinds
of bulbs, woodies,
perennials, vines

We-Du Nursery
Rt. 5, Box 724
Marion, NC 28752
catalog $2; uncommon
woodies, perennials

White Flower Farm
Box 50
Litchfield, CT 06759
catalog $5; woodies,
perennials, bulbs

Whitman Farms
3995 Gibson Rd., N.W.
Salem, OR 97304
catalog $1; woodies,
edibles

Gilbert H. Wild and Son, Inc.
Sarcoxie, MO 64862
catalog $3; perennials, peonies,
iris, Hemerocallis

Winterthur Plant Shop
Winterthur, DE 19735
free list; uncommon woodies

Woodlanders
1128 Colleton Ave.
Aiken, SC 29801
catalog $2; woodies,
hardy Passiflora

Yucca Do
P.O. Box 655
Waller, TX 77484
catalog $3; woodies, perennials

Credits

Thanks to all the gardeners and institutions who provided the subject matter for my photography:

American Horticultural Society, River Farm, Alexandria, VA

Atlanta Botanic Garden, Atlanta, GA

Ernesta and Fred Ballard, Philadelphia, PA

Breck's Bulbs, Peoria, IL

British Columbia, University of, Botanic Garden, Vancouver, BC

Burpee Seed Co., Warminster, PA

Brooklyn Botanic Garden, Brooklyn, NY

Butchart Gardens, Victoria, BC

Central Park, New York, NY

Chelsea Flower Show, London, England

Chicago Botanic Garden, Chicago, IL

Dorado Beach Hotel, Puerto Rico

El Junque (Rain Forest), Puerto Rico

Betsy Feuerstein, Memphis, TN

Lincoln and Helen Foster, Falls Village, CT

Golden Gate Park Conservatory, San Francisco, CA

Great Dixter Gardens, England

C.Z. Guest, Old Westbury, NY

Hope Hendler, New York, NY

Hidcote Manor Gardens, Gloucestershire, England

Hortus Bulborum, Holland

Michael Kartuz, Vista, CA

Keukenhof Gardens, Lisse, Holland

Live Oak Gardens, New Iberia, LA

Logee's Greenhouses, Danielson, CT

Longue Vue Gardens, New Orleans, PA

Longwood Gardens, Kennett Square, PA

Los Angeles State and County Arboretum, Arcadia, CA

Odette McMurrey, Houston, TX

James K. McNair, San Francisco, CA

Mercer Arboretum and Botanic Gardens, Humble, TX

Montreal Botanical Garden, Montreal, Quebec

Georgia and Eugene Mosier, Sewickley Heights, PA

The New York Botanical Garden, Bronx, NY

Old Westbury Gardens, Old Westbury, NY

Peckerwood Gardens, Waller, TX

Phipps Conservatory, Pittsburgh, PA

Adele Pieper, Houston, TX

Duncan and Kathy Pitney, NJ

Plum Creek Farm, Sharon, CT

Roger's Nursery, Corona Del Mar, CA

Royal Botanical Garden at Kew, London, England

Josephine Shanks, Houston, TX

Sissinghurst Castle Gardens, Kent, England

Strybing Arboretum, San Francisco, CA

Swan Island Dahlias, Canby, OR

Nikki Threlkeld, Vista, CA

Wakehurst Gardens, England

Wave Hill Gardens, Bronx, NY

Index

U.S.D.A. Plant Hardiness Zone Map

Average Annual Minimum Temperature

Temperature (°C)	Zone	Temperature (°F)
-45.6 and below	1	below -50
-45.6 and -45.5	2a	-45 to -50
-40.0 to -42.7	2b	-40 to -45
-37.3 to -40.0	3a	-35 to -40
-34.5 to -37.2	3b	-30 to -35
-31.7 to -34.4	4a	-25 to -30
-28.9 to -31.6	4b	-20 to -25
-26.2 to -28.8	5a	-15 to -20
-23.4 to -26.1	5b	-10 to -15
-20.6 to -23.3	6a	-5 to -10
-17.8 to -20.5	6b	0 to -5
-15.0 to -17.7	7a	5 to 0
-12.3 to -15.0	7b	10 to 5
-9.5 to -12.2	8a	15 to 10
-6.7 to -9.4	8b	20 to 15
-3.9 to -6.6	9a	25 to 20
-1.2 to -3.8	9b	30 to 25
1.6 to -1.1	10a	35 to 30
4.4 to 1.7	10b	40 to 45
4.5 and above	11	40 and above

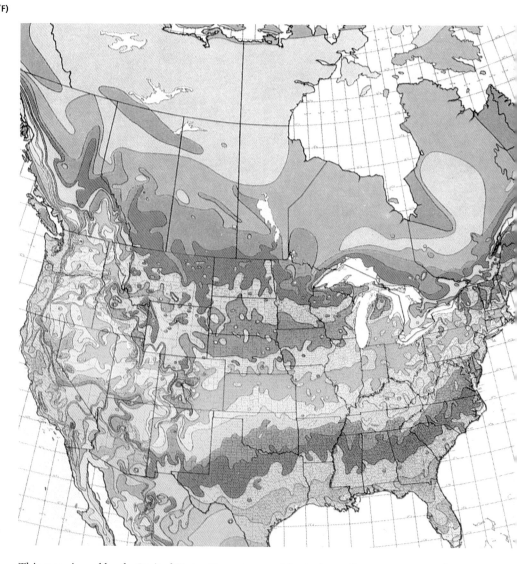

This map, issued by the United States Department of Agriculture, lists average annual minimum temperatures for each zone. It relates directly to the cold-hardiness of plants, but does not address the other extreme, high temperatures. Special considerations with regard to these matters are noted as appropriate throughout the pages of this book.
A new map, in preparation by the U.S.D.A. in cooperation with the American Horticultural Society, will treat equally matters of hot and cold and their effect on plants.